The Wrong Word Dictionary

CASTLE BOOKS

The Wrong Word Dictionary

By Dave Dowling
Illustrated by Corne

CASTLE BOOKS

This edition published in 2008 by

Castle Books ®

A division of Book Sales, Inc.
276 Fifth Ave., Suite 206
New York, NY 10001

This edition published by arrangement with and permission of
Marion Street Press, Inc.
PO Box 2249
Oak Park, IL 60303

Cover design by Anne Locascio
Illustrations by Corne

Library of Congress Cataloging-in-Publication Data:

Dowling, Dave, 1951-
      The wrong word dictionary: 2,000 most commonly confused words / by Dave
Dowling.
          p.   cm.
    1.   English language—Usage—Dictionaries. 2. English Language—Errors of
usage—Dictionaries. I. Title.

PE1464.D69 2005
423'.1—dc22

2004030536

ISBN-13: 978-0-7858-2408-4
ISBN-10: 0-7858-2408-1

Printed in the United States of America

To Mary and Tim

Preface

The difference between the almost right word and the right word is really a large matter — 'tis the difference between the lightning-bug and the lightning.

– Mark Twain

Unlike math and science, writing has very few absolutes. To that end, we're faced with making choices, and many times those choices are word choices. Since I began teaching technical and business writing in industry years ago, one lesson never grew old – an exercise on when to write the right word. Many writers confuse *complement* when they mean *compliment, compose* when they mean *comprise*, or *assume* when they mean *presume*. And hundreds of other mistaken word identities also exist. This quick reference aims to filter this confusion of words. Remember, writing is much easier to comprehend when the noise around it is eliminated.

Though not inclusive of all word pair mistakes, this book speaks to the common word choices that challenge us daily. This book consists of more than 900 entries and the meanings of more than 2,000 individual words or phrases. Much of the content is based on word problems I've witnessed during my 25 years of business writing as well as the misuse commonly found in the online and print media.

If you're looking for the basic sound alike words (*to, too, two,* etc.), you won't find them here. But you will find the basic pronoun possessives (*their, they're, there, who's* and *whose,* and *you're* and *your*) because they still give us problems. I've tried to eliminate obvious synonyms (*inedible* vs. *uneatable, simultaneous* vs. *concurrently, rare* vs. *scarce,* etc.) and include just word pairs where the word distinction is still important yet challenging.

Note that a few entries may seem trivial, and others may seem a bit obscure or obsolete. Still other entries may be showing word confusion caused only by the subtle misspelling of a word (*spade* vs. *spayed*, *cite* vs. *site*). But overall you'll find it a good mix of problem words (*among* vs. *between*, *flounder* vs. *founder*, *blatant* vs. *flagrant*). Also included are a few notes on phrases that often lead to problem writing (*between you and I*, *one of the only*, and others).

For each entry in this reference, the difference between the words is explained, and in most cases, a short and simple sentence example showing the correct usage is provided. The word definitions provided are intended strictly as guides and not dictionary definitions. They should help you differentiate between the words. Current dictionaries, popular writing books, and reputable style guides were among the many resources consulted for this book. The word list is arranged alphabetically according to the first word in the set.

Always think about the words you use. Accuracy in word choice is a key to effective communication. In your daily writing, try to make sure you apply the *right word* for the *right meaning*. By doing so, its effect can affect your writing in a positive way.

— *Dave Dowling*

Acknowledgments

This book would not have materialized without the sincere encouragement of my good friend Harry Dracon. After reading my weekly word tips, Harry strongly urged me to expand this idea into a book. I was reluctant at first because I doubted an audience existed for such a topic. I was wrong, and today I'm certainly glad I listened to a friend. Thank you, Harry, for all your inspiration, belief, and support. You were right to push me in this right word direction.

Whether it was ideas, constructive criticism, or encouragement when this project was in its online infancy, I must thank a few other people who influenced me on this word journey. I'm particularly grateful to Harold Sasnowitz, Vince Lozano, and Robert Hartwell Fiske for all their professional advice and expertise. Thanks, friends, for your generous time, and thanks for being there.

And a special thanks to Bruce Roberts, Ed Avis, and the staff at Marion Street Press, Inc. who used their word-processing pencils to edit these pages. Thanks friends for your expert editorial advice. You're pros who know prose.

Finally, a heartfelt thanks goes to my wife Mary and son Tim. Without their help, belief, and reassurance, this book would not exist. They're my best critics, my best friends, and the joy in my life.

The
Wrong
Word
Dictionary

A

By words the mind is excited and the spirit elated. – Aristophanes

A hold, Ahold

Ahold is not a word. **A hold** is standard English.
*I prefer e-mail, but another way to get **a hold** of me is by phone.*

À la mode, Alamode

À la mode refers to being served with ice cream.
*The restaurant was known for serving pie **à la mode** with every meal.*

Alamode refers to a thin silk usually found in scarfs and hoods.
*She complemented her winter outfit with a black **alamode** scarf.*

A long way, A long ways

A long way is the correct phrase.
*If you become bilingual, your career can go **a long way**.*

A part, Apart

A part refers to the union of something.
*Volunteering at the hospital has become **a part** of her routine.*

Apart refers to a separation in place, position, or time.
*If anything sets her **apart**, it's her volunteer work at the hospital.*

A ways

Incorrect phrase. The article **a** is singular; therefore, the word following **a** must also be singular (**way**).
*The Town Square Mall is **a** little **way** down the parkway.*

A while, Awhile

A while, a noun phrase, is used as the object of the prepositions *for* and *in*.
*Tom and Linda have decided to stay for **a while** in Otego.*
*In **a while**, Tom and Linda will leave Otego for good.*

Awhile is an adverb that means *for a time.*
*Tom and Linda are deciding whether to stay **awhile** in Otego.*

Abdicate, Abrogate, Arrogate

Abdicate means to give up, relinquish power, or renounce formally.
*By leaving the job, did Paul **abdicate** his rights to a pension?*

Abrogate means to abolish, cancel, or revoke something.
*Why are the politicians seeking to **abrogate** the agreement?*

Arrogate means to take, claim, or assume without any right.
*He **arrogated** to himself what should be in the company charter.*

Ability, Capacity

Ability refers to the power to do something.
*Some vitamins are said to have the **ability** to prevent colds.*

Capacity refers to the ability to hold or contain something.
*Madison Square Garden has a **capacity** of 20,000 seats.*

Abjure, Adjure

Abjure means to recant, renounce, or repudiate something.
*To the council's surprise, he **abjures** all rights to his citizenship.*

Adjure means to appeal, entreat, or order something.
*The club **adjures** its members to show respect at all times.*

Abnormal, Subnormal

Abnormal means deviating from the average.
*Joyce's **abnormal** powers of concentration enable her to score well.*

Subnormal means less than normal or below the average.
*His SAT scores are **subnormal** and not as high as he expected.*

About, Approximately

About refers to a rough estimate.
*We are **about** halfway through the class and enjoying every minute.*

Approximately refers to near accuracy.
*The college currently enrolls **approximately** 4,000 students.*

Abridged, Expurgated, Unabridged
Unabridged means in its full length or original content.
Abridged means abbreviated or condensed. **Expurgated** means objectionable material has been removed.

Abstemious, Abstinent
Abstemious means eating or drinking in moderation.
*Barb's **abstemious** habits probably ensure her a longer life.*

Abstinent means abstaining from something (food, drink, etc).
*The young men pledge to remain **abstinent** until age 21.*

Abstractedly, Abstractly
Abstractedly means not paying attention, preoccupied, or removed.
*He sat through the lecture gazing **abstractedly** out the window.*

Abstractly means hard to understand or unspecific.
*Without pictures, he could only **abstractly** describe the tool.*

Abstruse, Obtuse
Abstruse means complex, deep, or difficult to understand.
*To the average person, Einstein's theory of relativity is **abstruse**.*

Obtuse means dull witted, not too sharp, or slow to understand.
*I'm sorry if I'm being **obtuse**, but I do not understand the point.*

Abundant, Fulsome
Abundant refers to something profuse or of great quantity.
*She received **abundant** praise for her work with the deaf.*

Fulsome refers to something so excessive it causes offense or disgust.
*Unfortunately, the host gave the speaker a **fulsome** introduction.*

Abuse

Abuse, Misuse

Abuse means to use or treat something badly or wrongly.
*I hope Frank doesn't **abuse** the new car his parents bought him.*

Misuse means to use something for which it was not intended.
*The students often **misuse** the school computers to play games.*

Accede, Concede, Exceed

Accede means to take a position of authority or to yield.
*He may **accede** to the throne, but only after taking the oath.*
*I **accede** to your demands, as long as they are realistic.*

Concede means to accept reluctantly.
*Friends urged the candidate not to **concede** on election night.*

Exceed means to surpass.
*The product and service **exceed** our customer's expectations.*

Accept, Except

Accept means to admit, receive, or agree.
*I **accept** him to our organization with pleasure.*
*We **accept** your invitation to the ceremonies.*
*They **accept** the jury's verdict with no problem.*

Except as a preposition means *other than.*
*The student's grades are low in every subject **except** science.*

Except as a verb means to exclude something.
*If you **except** his math grades, Ryan has an impressive average.*

Access, Excess

Access refers to an increase, an outburst, or the ability to get something.
*Their winnings at the casino gave them an **access** of wealth.*
*What started as a small dispute turned into an **access** of rage.*
*We give certain users **access** to the secure web site.*

Excess refers to an overindulgence or surplus.
*Betty has an **excess** of property she would like to sell.*
*At the picnic, a few employees ate to **excess**.*

Accessary, Accessory

Accessory is the preferred spelling, but either is acceptable.

Accessible, Assessable

Accessible means capable of being approached, influenced, obtained, or understood.
*She works for an **accessible** supervisor whom everyone likes.*
*His technologies make TV **accessible** for the disabled.*
*The information is readily **accessible** to a nontechnical audience.*

*Sorry, we **accept** every card **except** Visa.*

Accident

Assessable means capable of being evaluated.
*The assessor classifies every item of **assessable** property.*

Accident, Incident, Mishap

Accident refers to an unforeseen event (good or bad).
*George's call about the job opening was just a lucky **accident**.*
*A flawed design contributed to the Chernobyl **accident**.*

Incident refers to a minor or simple occurrence (good or bad).
*The entire **incident** was recorded on video.*

Mishap refers to a minor unfortunate occurrence.
*Though no one was hurt, a **mishap** occurred during the parade.*

Accidentally, Accidently

Accidentally is the preferred spelling.
*If you **accidentally** delete the file, it is possible to restore it.*

Acclamation, Acclimation

Acclamation refers to an oral vote or praise of some kind.
*The board passed by **acclamation** a motion to fund the plan.*
*The Honor Society appreciated the **acclamation** of the principal.*

Acclimation refers to adapting to a new climate or environment.
*Her **acclimation** to the cold weather took longer than expected.*

Accord, Accordance

Accord refers to an agreement or settlement.
*Congress arrived at a unanimous **accord** on the amendment.*

Accordance refers to conformity to regulations.
*My plan is in **accordance** with the Stock Exchange Regulations.*

Accuse, Allege

Accuse means to blame or charge someone with wrongdoing.
*No one **accuses** him of mishandling the funds.*

Allege means to claim something not yet proven.
*The investigator **alleges** the investors were tricked by a scam.*

Acetic, Aesthetic, Ascetic

Acetic refers to things having an acid characteristic.
*Because of its **acetic** taste, there's a chance the juice is old.*

Aesthetic refers to artistic or beautiful things.
*The architect designs buildings with **aesthetic** ideas in mind.*

Ascetic refers to a person austere in appearance, manner, or attitude.
*He lives an **ascetic** existence, supporting himself on a farm.*

Acidulous, Assiduous

Acidulous means tart or sour in taste or manner.
*Her **acidulous** wit makes her unpopular with some employees.*

Assiduous means diligent or persistent.
*He is **assiduous** in visiting the sick, wherever they live.*

Acknowledgment, Acknowledgement

Acknowledgment without the second e is preferred in American usage.
*Applicants are now receiving **acknowledgment** letters.*

Acme, Climax

Acme is the highest point.
*The **acme** of the classical piano recital was Sharon's song.*

Climax is the point of greatest intensity.
*The **climax** of the night's events is the colorful fireworks display.*

Acquaintance, Friend

An **acquaintance** is a person one knows. A **friend** is a person one knows, likes, and trusts.
*Joe is an example of an **acquaintance** who became a **friend**.*

Acquiesce in, Acquiesce to, Acquiesce with

Acquiesce means to consent or comply without protest. When **acquiesce** takes a preposition, it is usually **in**.
*His government can't **acquiesce in** the invasion of that country.*

Acquiesce with the preposition **to** is uncommon, but acceptable.
*Gracie, Audrey, and Patrick **acquiesced to** their parents' wishes.*

Acquiesced with is considered obsolete.

Acquitted from, Acquitted of

Acquitted of is the preferred phrase.
*The suspect is **acquitted of** all charges relating to the case.*

Acute, Chronic

Concerning physical condition:

Acute refers to an extremely severe or sharp condition.
*While playing basketball, he experienced **acute** stomach pain.*

Chronic refers to a lingering or prolonged condition.
*Through stretching exercises, one can relieve **chronic** back pain.*

Ad, Add

Ad is the shortened form of **ad**vertisement.
*We placed an **ad** in the classified section of Sunday's paper.*

Add means to total something or contribute to something.
*If we **add** every golf score, we played better than many teams.*
*Let's **add** more sugar to the lemonade.*

Ad nauseam, Ad nauseum

This much overused phrase is often spelled incorrectly as **ad nauseum**.

Adage, Axiom

Adage refers to a saying that has obtained acceptance.
*"Nothing ventured, nothing gained" is an **adage** many use.*

Axiom refers to a universally accepted rule or principle.
*This **axiom** is consistent with the rules of set theory.*

Adapt, Adept, Adopt

Adapt means to adjust, change, or make suitable.
*Christian **adapts** well to new working environments.*

Adept means to be skilled at something.
*Among other things, Frances is **adept** at shuffling cards.*

Adopt means to accept or to take as your own.
*Because of its merits, we shall **adopt** your proposal immediately.*
*Our son, who is now 18, was **adopted** 10 weeks after his birth.*

Addenda, Agenda

Addenda (plural) are additions to something.
*The **addenda** to the manual give the hardware requirements.*

Agenda is a schedule or list of things to do.
*The **agenda** for this year's seminar is interesting and varied.*

Addition, Edition

Addition is something added.
*Jane and Kerry built an **addition** to their camp last summer.*

Edition is one complete issue of a publication.
*That story should be in the newspaper's latest **edition**.*

Adduce, Deduce, Deduct

Adduce means to cite as an example or proof in an argument.
*The attorneys did not try to **adduce** fresh evidence in the case.*

Deduce means to conclude from a rule, principle, or reasoning.
*Brian **deduced** from the laws of physics that the plane would fly.*

Deduct means to take away from.
*Some believe too many taxes are **deducted** from their wages.*

Adhere, Cohere

Adhere means to stick fast, to be devoted, or to carry out a plan.
*Using that glue, the wallpaper should **adhere** to the wall quickly.*
*They have **adhered** to that particular faith for many years.*
*We are taking your advice and **adhering** to the revised plan.*

Cohere means to hold together as part of the same thing.
*Generally, the film's subplots failed to **cohere**.*

Adherence, Adherents

Adherence refers to faithful commitment.
*His **adherence** to the corporation's goals was never in doubt.*

Adherents refer to advocates or supporters.
*Congress passed a law that pleased **adherents** of tax reform.*

Adieu, Ado, Á deux

Adieu means goodbye.
*Since joining the health club, they bid **adieu** to bad eating habits.*

Ado means bother, fuss, or trouble.
*"Husband, let's follow, to see the end of this **ado**." –* The Taming of the Shrew

Á deux means to involve two people in a private or intimate nature.
*The inn featured dining **à deux**, private porches, and cut flowers.*

Adjacent, Adjoining

Adjacent means next to, but without physical contact.
*The basketball arena is directly **adjacent** to the team's hotel.*

Adjoining means having a common point of contact.
*The basketball team players have **adjoining** rooms in the hotel.*

Adjudicate, Arbitrate, Mediate

Adjudicate means to act as a judge in disputes.
*The department has jurisdiction to **adjudicate** all of the appeals.*

Arbitrate means to make a neutral judgment.
*Ken willingly agrees to **arbitrate** the contract dispute.*

Mediate means to bring parties together or reconcile differences.
*Ed is attempting to **mediate** the differences between the teams.*

Administer, Administrate

Administer is the proper verb form for *administration* or *administrator*.
*They wondered which lawyer would **administer** the estate.*

Advance, Advancement

Advance refers to improvement, movement, or progress.
*Her research resulted in an **advance** in molecular biology.*

Advancement refers to promotion.
*The fund is for the **advancement** of science and technology.*

Adverse, Averse

Adverse means difficult or unfavorable.
*The rule could have an **adverse** effect on our business.*

Averse means opposed to.
*The public relations director is **averse** to our business proposal.*

Adversity, Diversity

Adversity refers to affliction, hardship, or misfortune.
*After a year of financial **adversity**, the company rebounded well.*

Diversity refers to an assortment or variety of things.
*To add **diversity** to your portfolio, consider this investment.*

Advert, Avert

Advert means to call attention to or refer to something.
*The speaker **adverted** to a point she had made earlier.*

Avert means to prevent or ward off something.
*To avoid any delays, management wants to **avert** a strike.*

Advise, Inform

Advise means to give advice, counsel, or suggestions.
*We will **advise** you on proper use of the new printer.*

Inform means to communicate information.
*The teacher will **inform** the students when the tests are graded.*

Advisedly, Intentionally

Advisedly means deliberately or with careful consideration.
*She chose her words to the media **advisedly**.*

Intentionally means with intent or purpose.
The author intentionally left his phone off the hook.

Adviser, Advisor

Adviser is the preferred spelling, but either is acceptable.

Aerial, Ariel

Aerial refers to a radio antenna or something else that reaches into the air.
Before cable TV, many people put TV aerials on their roofs.
Aerial photography is becoming one of her favorite pastimes.

Ariel refers to a kind of gazelle or the brightest moon of Uranus.
The ariel gazelle is under two feet tall and lives in the desert.
Much of Ariel's surface is pitted with craters.

Aerie, Airy, Eerie

Aerie means nest.
Have you ever been to the mountains and seen an eagle's aerie?

Airy means breezy.
The airy conditions at the Jersey shore always keep us cool.

Eerie means spooky.
The séance we attended was an eerie experience for everybody.

Affect, Effect

The verb **affect** means to influence or change.
The moon and sun can affect the ocean's tides.

The verb **effect** means to bring about or accomplish.
The new CEO effected a few minor changes to the company.

The noun **effect** means result.
One effect of the drought was a skimpy corn crop.

Memory hook: If you **affect** something, you can have an **effect** on it.

Affectation, Affection

Affectation refers to artificial, exaggerated, or false behavior.
Forget the vocabulary affectations. We prefer plain language.

Affection refers to fondness toward someone.
The club has a deep affection and respect for that family.

Affidavid, Affidavit

Affidavit is the correct word.

Affinity, Eternity, Infinity

Affinity means a close relationship or connection.
The organization has a strong affinity for environmental issues.

Eternity means unending time or forever.
The pastor told the mourners that Jill would live an eternity.

Infinity means unlimited quantity, space, or time.
From the ground, that highway appears to go on for an infinity.

Afflatus, Flatus

Afflatus refers to divine inspiration, and **flatus** refers to gas generated by the intestine.

Afflict, Inflict

Afflict means to cause suffering for someone or something.
The disease first afflicted people who were not vaccinated.

Inflict means to cause by aggressive action.
The truck hit a parked car and inflicted severe damage to it.

Affluent, Effluent

Affluent refers to the rich.
Joan jokingly claims she is from an affluent background.

Effluent refers to a river, stream, or lake that flows out.
The farmer uses water from that effluent to water his garden.

Aforesaid

Aforesaid, meaning *stated previously,* should be restricted to legal writing.

After all, Afterall

After all is always two words.

Afterward, Afterwards

Afterward is preferred in American usage.

Aggravate, Irritate

Aggravate means to make something worse or more severe.
*Research shows that dust can **aggravate** lung problems.*

Irritate means to annoy.
*His management style **irritates** us.*
*Vitamin C, aspirin, and potassium can **irritate** the esophagus.*

Aggression, Egression

Aggression refers to hostility.
*The wild animals showed **aggression** toward their captors.*

Egression refers to the act of emerging.
*The hypnotist showed the man an **egression** into a future life.*

Agnostic, Atheist

An **agnostic** feels the existence of God cannot be proved or disproved. An **atheist** completely denies the existence of God.

Agree to, Agree with

Agree to means to concede to something.
*We hope the local officials can **agree to** a compromise this year.*

Agree with means to be in accord with something.
*Both parties **agree with** each other on the new spending plan.*

Agreeance, Agreement

Agreement is the preferred word. **Agreeance** is an obsolete word.

Aid, Aide

Aid refers to assistance.
*Animal **Aid** is one of the oldest animal rights groups in the world.*

Aide refers to a helper.
*The congressional **aide** says the Senator is unavailable now.*

*The student was grateful for the **aid** the teacher's **aide** provided.*

25

Ailment, Aliment

Ailment refers to an illness.
*The skin **ailment** develops due to a bacterial infection.*

Aliment refers to supplying with sustenance, such as food or moral support.
*The law requires the family be supplied with different **aliments**.*

Aisle, Isle

Aisle is a passageway between seats, traffic, or other things.
*Two by two the wedding party marched down the **aisle**.*

Isle refers to a small island.
*The **Isle** of Wight was a famous 1970 concert venue in England.*

All, Alls

Use **all**, never **alls**.
***All** (not **alls**) you hear them talk about are their careers.*

All I know is, Alls I know is

All I know is the correct phrase.
***All I know is** that the strict diet affected my cholesterol levels.*

All kinds of

Avoid using this awkward colloquialism. Use *many* or *much* instead.

All of a sudden, All of the sudden

All of a sudden is the correct phrase.

All over, Allover

All over means finished or everywhere.
*The job of wallpapering the dining room was finally **all over**.*
*The paint spilled **all over** the floor.*

Allover means covering the entire surface of something.
*The wallpaper had an **allover** pattern of flowers and trees.*

All ready, Already

All ready means totally prepared.
*Steve tells us the system is **all ready** and available to use.*

Already means *by this time* or *so soon*.
*It was **already** noon before Steve could restart the system.*

All right, Alright

All right must always be two words. **Alright** is considered a nonstandard word. Avoid its use.
*It's certainly **all right** to be nervous before an important speech.*

All the farther, As far as

As far as is the preferred phrase.
*Is that **as far as** (not **all the farther**) you drove today?*

All together, Altogether

All together means in one complete group.
*The reports are **all together** on the conference room table.*

Altogether means completely, entirely, or totally.
*The presentation is **altogether** too long for next week's meeting.*

All ways, Always

All ways means by every way or method.
*Ensure they look **all ways** before crossing the intersection.*

Always means *all the time* or *forever*.
*We will **always** remember the good things they did for the poor.*

Allay, Alleviate

Allay means to make less or to delete altogether.
*To **allay** the oil shortage, scientists are developing other fuels.*

Alleviate means to relieve something unpleasant or painful.
*Simple aspirin can quickly **alleviate** some of your discomfort.*

Allergenic, Allogeneic

Allergenic refers to a substance that can cause an allergy.
*He is testing the lotion to see if it causes **allergenic** problems.*

Allogeneic refers to belonging to the same species but being genetically different.
*The hospital offers **allogeneic** stem cell transplantation.*

Alliterate, Illiterate

Alliterate means to arrange words with a repeating initial consonant sound.
*Most tongue-twisters in modern English **alliterate**. (<u>P</u>eter <u>P</u>iper <u>p</u>icked a <u>p</u>eck of <u>p</u>ickled <u>p</u>eppers.)*

Illiterate refers to the inability to read or write or the lack of knowledge in a certain subject.
*Sadly, 20 percent of their state's adults are **illiterate**.*
*Some of the students were computer **illiterate**.*

Allot, Alot, A lot

Allot means to allocate or share something.
*The education budget **allots** money for reading programs.*

Alot is not a word.

A lot is always two words.
A lot of people today are doing business on the Internet.

Allude, Elude, Refer

Allude means to hint or refer to indirectly.
*The memo did **allude** to past equipment failures and problems.*

Elude means to avoid or escape.
*After the hit, the base runner tried to **elude** the shortstop's tag.*

Refer means to make direct reference to something.
*If you have other questions, **refer** to the charts for more data.*

Allusion, Delusion, Illusion

Allusion is a reference to something.
*Emma makes **allusions** to her favorite books and authors.*

Delusion is a mistaken belief or opinion.
*He has a **delusion** that man never set foot on the moon.*

Illusion is a deceptive appearance.
*The optical **illusion** is actually an effect of perspective.*

Almost, Most

When you want to say *nearly all,* use **almost**.
*Kerry touches base with work **almost** (not **most**) every day of his vacation.*

Aloud, Out loud

Aloud is standard English. **Out loud** is considered colloquial.
*The teacher always enjoys reading **aloud** to the class.*

Altar, Alter

Altar refers to the platform at the front of a church or temple.
*They keep the daily prayer book on the church's **altar**.*

Alter means to change.
*The judge may **alter** her decision on cameras in the courtroom.*

Alteration, Altercation, Alternation

Alteration is a change.
*Some scientists believe gene **alteration** may raise cancer risk.*

Altercation is an argument, dispute, or fight.
*Play stopped because of an **altercation** in the outfield stands.*

Alternation is a constant back and forth change.
*The doctor experimented with the **alternation** of two remedies.*

Alterior, Ulterior

Ulterior, as in **ulterior** motive, is the correct word.

Alternate, Alternative

Alternate, as an adjective, means every other one. As a verb it means to change from one to another.
Every **alternate** *Friday, Joe, Doug, and Eric meet for golf.*
He **alternates** *between his five wood and driver off the tee.*

An **alternative** is another option.
The **alternative** *is to leave early before the afternoon traffic.*

Although, Whereas

Although means *in spite of the fact that.*
Although *your membership expired, we will honor your request.*

Whereas means *to the contrary.*
The first lecture was boring, **whereas** *the next one was fun.*

Alumna, Alumnus

Alumna is a former female student (plural is *alumnae*).
Alumnus is a former male student (plural is *alumni*).

Amateur, Novice

Amateur refers to someone who does an activity as a pastime.
Arnold was an exceptional **amateur** *before turning professional.*

A **novice** is a beginner.
When it comes to playing golf or tennis, he is just a **novice**.

Ambiguous, Ambivalent, Indifferent

Ambiguous means unclear or subject to interpretation.
The candidate is so **ambiguous** *that few understand his platform.*

Ambivalent means having mixed feelings or being uncertain.
He is **ambivalent** *about returning to college for more courses.*

Indifferent means being apathetic or showing no concern.
The legislature remains **indifferent** *about building a new library.*

Amend, Emend

Amend means to add to or change.
*The surveys prove it; it's time to **amend** our society's charter.*

Emend means to make changes or corrections, specifically to text.
*Before the next edition, the editor wants to **emend** the book.*

Amiable, Amicable

Amiable means agreeable and easy to deal with, and is applied to a person.
*Ty is an **amiable** person with whom I enjoy playing golf.*

Amicable means good willed or friendly, and is used to describe relations between people or other entities.
*France maintains an **amicable** relationship with that country.*

Among, Amongst

Among is preferred in American English.

Among, Between

Among is used for relationships involving more than two.
*The managers agree **among** themselves that the solution failed.*

Between is usually used for relationships involving only two, but may be used for more when the items are distinctly separate.
*Clean your cleats **between** the second and third innings.*
*The choice for best golfer of the 1960s is **between** Arnold, Gary, and Jack.*
*The plane crash-landed in the field **between** the four houses.*

Amoral, Immoral

Amoral means without morality.
*They are known to be **amoral**, with no sense of right or wrong.*

Immoral means contrary to established moral standards.
*Though it is popular, some people may find the book **immoral**.*

Amount, Number

Amount refers to things that cannot be counted individually.
*Furnishing a new office requires a great **amount** of time.*

Number refers to countable things.
*The tenants bought a large **number** of PCs for the office.*

Ample, Enough

Ample means more than adequate in capacity, scope, or size.
*You have **ample** opportunity to talk with prospective clients.*

Enough means adequate or sufficient to satisfy a need.
*Make sure you have **enough** RAM to run the program.*

Amuse, Bemuse

Amuse means to entertain.
*His jokes still **amuse** us, even though we've heard them all.*

Bemuse means to bewilder, confuse, or stupefy.
*The change in tactics appears to **bemuse** our opponents.*

Analysis, Analyzation

Analysis is the preferred and less pompous word to use.

Analyst, Annalist

Analyst is someone skilled at studying or analyzing problems.
*The systems **analyst** spends much time at the computer.*

Annalist is someone who writes historical records.
*The **annalist** recounted the events that shaped World War II.*

Anchors away, Anchors aweigh

Anchors aweigh is the correct phrase. The word *weigh*
originates from an old word meaning heave, hoist, or raise.
Aweigh means something, in this case an anchor, has been
raised.
*The captain called **anchors aweigh** as the ship prepared to
leave.*

Androgenous, Androgynous
Androgenous refers to producing male offspring.
The chromosome prompts the formation of androgenous embryoids.

Androgynous refers to having both male and female characteristics.
The androgynous offspring surprised the researchers.

Anecdote, Antidote
Anecdote is a short account (usually funny) about an incident.
Alex told us many amusing anecdotes about his time in college.

Antidote is a medicine or remedy for fighting poison or disease.
The doctor prescribes antidotes to counteract any poison.

Annihilate, Decimate
Annihilate means to destroy something completely.
The company uses a spray to annihilate the lawn weeds.

Decimate literally means to destroy one tenth of something, but is commonly used to mean destroying a large part of something.
The strong weed killer could decimate many parts of the lawn.

Annunciate, Enunciate
Annunciate, a rare word, means to announce or proclaim.
In the event of trouble, the system annunciates an alarm.

Enunciate means to pronounce, articulate, or set forth precisely.
The statements enunciate their position on conservation issues.

Antagonist, Protagonist
Antagonist refers to an adversary or opponent.
Once close friends, they became antagonists later in life.

Protagonist is a leading character in a play, novel, or story.
The protagonist in tonight's play also serves as the narrator.

Protagonist, meaning a proponent, is becoming more common.
Tony is a protagonist of solar energy and reduced emissions.

33

Ante, Anti

Ante means before or in front of something.
*The abbreviation A.M. stands for **ante** meridian (before noon).*

Anti means against or opposed to something.
*To combat the poison effectively, the doctor needs an **anti**toxin.*

Anticipate, Expect

Anticipate means to foresee and prepare for something.
*The college **anticipates** a large enrollment jump next year.*

Expect means to look forward to a likely occurrence.
*The college **expects** most of the senior class to get job offers.*

Anticlimactic, Anticlimatic

Anticlimactic is the correct word.

Anxious, Eager

Anxious means nervous, worried, or filled with anxiety.
*Harry is **anxious** about his final grades in math and science.*

Eager means looking forward to or earnestly longing.
*Greg is **eager** to see how well he did in math and science.*

Any more, Anymore

Any more means some more.
*Annie and Mary do not want **any more** problems with their cars.*

Anymore means now.
*Our friends do not live here **anymore**, and we miss them.*

Any one, Anyone

Any one refers to any single person or thing.
*Did you listen to **any one** of the new holiday CD releases?*

Anyone refers to any person.
*Did **anyone** in the class see the solar eclipse yesterday?*

Any time, Anytime

Any time means one of many times.
Any time the team scores, the fans are delighted.

Anytime means at any time.
*They can attend the meeting **anytime** they wish.*

Any way, Anyway

Any way means by a choice of methods.
*Joe tries to improve his car's performance **any way** he can.*

Anyway means in any case or nevertheless.
Anyway, George is attending the concert despite his late start.

Anyways, Anywheres

Always use **anyway** and **anywhere**.

Apportion, Portion, Proportion

Apportion means to distribute or divide.
*The attorney wants to **apportion** the shares of stock evenly.*

Portion, as a noun, means a limited amount of something.
*The family wants to leave a big **portion** of the estate to charity.*

Portion, as a verb, is a synonym for *apportion* (distribute or divide).
*The family wants to **portion** part of the large estate to charity.*

Proportion means a ratio of one thing to another.
*The **proportion** of golfers to tennis players increases every year.*

Appose, Oppose

Appose means to place near one another or to juxtapose.
*The box's edges should be **apposed** and slightly turned in.*

Oppose means to act adversely or in opposition.
*The Senator says he would **oppose** the bill if put to a vote.*

Apposite, Opposite

Apposite means appropriate, pertinent, or suitable.
*Her style of acting and singing is **apposite** for the lead part.*

Opposite means altogether different or to the contrary.
*The producer has an **opposite** view about casting the lead.*

Appraise, Apprise

Appraise means to estimate, evaluate, or judge something.
*Have someone **appraise** your ring; then properly insure it.*

Apprise means to advise or inform.
*Please **apprise** the accused person of his constitutional rights.*

Appropriate, Apropos

Appropriate means suitable or fitting.
*The timing of John's promotion could not be more **appropriate**.*

Apropos means in regard to, incidentally, or relevant.
***Apropos** next week's meeting, now we cannot attend.*
***Apropos**, where is the schedule you promised us a week ago?*

Apt, Likely

Apt refers to a habitual tendency.
*Religious people are **apt** to pray and attend services regularly.*

Likely refers to a high probability.
*It's **likely** we will see our grandchildren over the holidays.*

Arc, Ark

Arc refers to something shaped with a curved or bowed line.
*In geometry, a segment of a curve is called an **arc**.*

Ark refers to a large, flat-bottomed boat.
*In the Old Testament, Noah built an **ark** for survival.*

Arctic, Artic
Always use **arctic**, not **artic**, as in **Arctic** Circle.

Area, Aria
Area refers to a region or section.
*To help us place you, what **area** of engineering is your specialty?*

Aria refers to a solo vocal piece.
*When the lead tenor finished his **aria**, they graciously applauded.*

Arraignment, Indictment
Arraignment is formally calling a defendant to answer a charge.
*The judge postponed the **arraignment** for a week.*

Indictment is formally charging a defendant with a crime.
*The grand jury handed up an **indictment** against five people.*

Arrant, Errant
Arrant means confirmed, downright, or extreme.
*Many of us found the story nothing short of **arrant** nonsense.*

Errant means wandering or roving.
*Ray's **errant** tee shot on the last hole cost him the tournament.*

Arrhythmic, Eurhythmic
Arrhythmic refers to lacking rhythm or the regularity of rhythm.
*During the hospitalization phase, slight **arrhythmic** disorders registered in 10 patients.*

Eurhythmic refers to the art of graceful and harmonious movement (dancing).
*The class includes **eurhythmic** and choreography techniques.*

Arthroscopic, Orthoscopic
Arthroscopic is the correct word.
*Her injured right knee required immediate **arthroscopic** surgery.*

Artisan, Artist, Artiste

Artisan refers to one skilled in a trade.
*Ed is an accomplished **artisan** whose passion is wood furniture.*

Artist refers to anyone engaged in the fine or performing arts.
*Marcel Marceau, a pantomime **artist**, was born in 1923.*

Artiste refers to an entertainer or anyone skilled in a special craft.
*The chef at Lake Mohonk is considered a real **artiste**.*

As, Like

As is a conjunction and is followed by a subject and verb.
*In the cold winter, he hibernates **as** a bear does.*

Like is a preposition and should be followed by an object.
*In the cold winter, he hibernates **like** a bear.*

As if, As though

Either phrase is acceptable, but grammarians prefer **as though**.
*You describe the film's details **as though** you have seen it.*

As time passed, As time progressed

Use **as time passed** because time does not *progress*.
***As time passed**, the animal became more domesticated.*

Ascent, Assent

Ascent means an upward climb or any movement upward.
*The mountain's slight **ascent** requires little climbing experience.*

Assent means to agree or concur with something.
*The teacher **assented** to accepting Jessica's late paper.*

Ascribe, Subscribe

Ascribe means to attribute to a source or author.
*Though this statement is usually **ascribed** to our president, it was actually written by a reporter.*

Subscribe means to agree with or to give assent.
*Many people do not **subscribe** to these conspiracy theories.*

Assay, Essay

Assay, a verb, means to evaluate or analyze something.
*Take time to **assay** the information before drawing a conclusion.*

Essay, as a verb, means to make an attempt.
*The baby boy **essayed** a few wobbly steps last week.*

Essay, as a noun, is a short composition expressing an author's opinion.
*Pat has to write an **essay** on Tolstoy for her literature class.*

Assert, Claim

Assert means to state or express firmly.
*The party's leader **asserts** she could not support the proposal.*

Claim means to demand or ask for as one's own.
*It is his birthday, so Larry is **claiming** the first piece of cake.*

Assume, Presume

Assume means to take for granted without evidence.
*Though it is common, do not **assume** fluoride is in your water.*

Presume means to take for granted, usually because evidence exists.
*The van is being serviced, so we **presume** it is not running well.*

Assure, Ensure, Insure

Assure means to make confident or promise something.
*I **assure** you the package is in the mail and delivery is imminent.*

Ensure means to make certain something will happen.
*Mailing the package by Friday **ensures** a Tuesday delivery.*

Insure means to buy insurance.
*Because of its value and size, we **insured** the package.*

At least, Leastways

Leastways is awkward. Use **at least**.
*That's not much of an achievement, **at least** (not **leastways**) not for him.*

Attaché, Briefcase

An **attaché** is a slim carrying case designed for carrying mainly paperwork. A **briefcase** is a larger carrying case that comes in varying sizes and shapes and is designed to carry more than just paperwork.

Attain, Obtain

Attain means to accomplish something.
*We wish Scott well in striving to **attain** his educational goals.*

Obtain means to get possession of something.
*Scott is determined to **obtain** his doctorate degree by next year.*

Auger, Augur

Auger refers to a tool for drilling holes.
*To drill holes for deck supports, Andy uses an electric **auger**.*

Augur means to predict or to be a sign of something.
*Recent developments could **augur** change for the car industry.*

Augment, Supplement

Augment means to increase in size, degree, or effect.
*Some people **augment** their income with Internet businesses.*

Supplement, as a verb, means to add something or make up for a deficiency.
*The doctor told Laura to **supplement** her diet with vitamins.*

Supplement, as a noun, means something added.
*The new part-time job was a **supplement** to her full-time job.*

Aural, Oral

Aural refers to the ear or to the sense of hearing.
*The young class has more success learning by **aural** methods.*

Oral refers to things of the mouth.
*The hygienist always does an **oral** exam before the cleaning.*

Authentication, Authentification
The correct spelling is **authentication**.
*We signed a certificate of **authentication** for the buyer.*

Authoritarian, Authoritative
Authoritarian means requiring absolute obedience to authority.
*Does **authoritarian** government always involve censorship?*

Authoritative means approved by a proper authority.
*The nutritionist is writing an **authoritative** guide to eating well.*

Avalanche, Landslide
An **avalanche** refers to snow, rocks, or other debris coming down a mountainside. A **landslide** is an entire mountainside coming down.

Avert, Avoid, Divert
Avert means to prevent or ward off something.
*Moderate exercise and diet can sometimes **avert** weight gain.*

Avoid is to shun or stay clear of something.
*Tom tries to **avoid** the tough questions at a press conference.*

Divert is to turn aside, distract, or turn from one course to another.
*You can **divert** an incoming call to a cell phone with that feature.*

Avocation, Evocation, Vocation
Avocation refers to something one does outside of work.
*As we imagined, Celeste's true **avocation** is gardening.*

Evocation means spiritually summoning something through the power of the mind.
*"The **evocation** of that better spirit." – M. Arnold*

Vocation refers to a profession, principal endeavor, or livelihood.
*Their **vocation** is responding to other people's needs.*

Avow, Vouch

Avow means admitting or declaring something publicly.
I avow that the education at Potsdam State is excellent.

Vouch means supporting the claims of something or someone.
I can vouch for her dedication, honesty, and sincerity.

Award, Reward

Award refers to something given as a prize.
John received an award for his antique tractor display.

Reward refers to something given for a good deed or service.
The firefighter received a reward for saving the child's life.

Axel, Axle

Axel refers to a difficult jump in figure skating (named after Norwegian figure skater Axel Paulsen). **Axle** refers to a shaft on which a wheel or set of wheels revolves.

Axiom, Axion

Axiom is an established truth, rule of law, or principle.
This axiom treats crime as a wrong done to another person not breaking the law.

Axion is a hypothetical particle of matter with no charge or spin and small mass.
One can identify this energy density as a bunch of axion particles found in galaxies.

B

The ill and unfitting choice of words wonderfully obstructs the understanding. — Francis Bacon

Backward, Backwards
Backward is preferred in American usage.

Bad, Badly
Bad is an adjective describing nouns or pronouns.
*Our family has a **bad** feeling about the whole thing.*
*John felt **bad** about missing Karen's surprise party.*

Badly is an adverb.
*Despite few rehearsals, the band is not playing **badly**.*

Baited, Bated
Baited means to entice or lure something.
*We **baited** the mousetrap with peanut butter.*

Bated means to lessen the force or intensity of something.
*The team waited with **bated** breath to see who won the game.*

Baleful, Baneful
Baleful refers to something that menaces or foreshadows evil.
*The teacher's **baleful** look helped silence the noisy students.*

Baneful refers to something harmful or destructive.
*The virus is having **baneful** effects on the farmer's cattle.*

Baloney, Bologna
Baloney is nonsense; **bologna** is sausage or lunch meat.

Baluster, Banister
A **baluster** is a short pillar that supports a handrail.
*The **balusters** on the deck were secured with small screws.*

Barb wire

A **banister** is the handrail on a staircase.
*We slid down the **banister** when we were children.*

Barb wire, Barbed wire, Bob wire
Though variations exist, the correct phrase is **barbed wire**.
*They replaced the **barbed wire** with a new type of barrier.*

Barbarism, Barbarity
Barbarism is a crude or rude act or an incorrect expression of words.
*Reputable magazines would never tolerate such **barbarisms**.*

Barbarity refers to savage brutality or cruelty in actions.
*Accounts of the dictator's **barbarity** shocked many countries.*

Basement, Cellar
A **basement** is the substructure or foundation of a building. A **cellar** is an underground shelter or space.

Batter, Dough
Batter is a thin mixture of flour and liquid (usually poured).
*Brian is whipping up some **batter** for more blueberry pancakes.*

Dough is a thick mixture of flour, liquid, and other things.
*To raise money for her class, she sold frozen cookie **dough**.*

Bazaar, Bizarre
Bazaar refers to a market where miscellaneous goods are sold.
*Nancy and Joan traveled to a local **bazaar** to scout antiques.*

Bizarre means strange, weird, or out of the ordinary.
*His **bizarre** behavior disrupts the entire class.*

Be sure and, Be sure to
Be sure to is the correct phrase.
*Please **be sure to** leave an e-mail address and phone number.*

*Jane found a pair of **bizarre** boots at the church **bazaar**.*

Because of, Due to

Because of refers to cause and effect.
Because of the band canceling, ticket holders are quite upset.

Due to should be used with a linking verb (*is, are, was*, etc.).
*The band's cancellation is **due to** poor ticket sales.*

Beckon call, Beck and call

Beck and call is the correct phrase. The word *beck* is a shortened form of *beckon*, which means to make a mute signal or gesture to call someone over.
*Unlike major newspapers, they don't have a research team at their **beck and call**.*

Behest, Request

Behest refers to an authoritative command or urging.
*At his **behest**, we made an appointment to see the dentist today.*

Request means to ask for something.
*The dentist **requests** that we try to avoid hard candy.*

Being as, Being that

Avoid these phrases in writing. Use **because** instead.
Because my car broke down, I missed my starting time.

Bemuse, Amuse

See entry for **Amuse, Bemuse**.

Benefactor, Beneficiary

Benefactor refers to someone who provides a gift.
*The university recognizes that Jim is a long-time **benefactor**.*

Beneficiary refers to someone who receives something.
*Tanya was the **beneficiary** of several research grants.*

Beside, Besides

Beside as a preposition means *next to* or *compared to*.
*The commissioner sat **beside** him at the awards dinner.*

Besides as a preposition means *in addition to* or *otherwise*.
***Besides** winning the math award, Jane is on the honor roll.*
*Who **besides** me likes his latest book?*

Besides as an adverb means *moreover*.
***Besides**, Al needs more than expensive clubs to lower his score.*

Between, Among

See entry for **Among, Between**.

Between you and I, Between you and me

Always use **between you and me**.
All prepositions, such as *between*, take pronouns in the
objective case (*it, her, him, me, them, us, you*) not in the
nominative case (*he, I, it, she, they, we, you*) or possessive case
(*her, hers, his, its, mine, my, our, ours, their, theirs, your, yours*).
*Just **between you and me**, we are having a party for the family.*

Biannual, Biennial

Biannual, a synonym for *semiannual*, means twice a year.
*Donna and John make **biannual** visits to North Carolina.*

Biennial means once every two years.
*The car registration is due for its **biennial** renewal.*

Bilateral, Multilateral, Unilateral

Bilateral, meaning two-sided, refers to two agreeing entities.
*The city has a **bilateral** agreement with the sports arena.*

Multilateral, meaning many-sided, refers to more than two agreeing entities.
*The company has a **multilateral** agreement with all four firms.*

Unilateral, meaning one-sided, refers to an entity acting alone.
*We have a **unilateral** agreement on free trade with that country.*

Bimonthly, Semimonthly

Bimonthly means occurring every two months.
*We bought the refreshments for the **bimonthly** status meeting.*

Semimonthly means occurring twice a month.
*Our **semimonthly** reports are due the first and third Friday of each month.*

Note: The same rules apply to *biweekly, biyearly, semiweekly,* and *semiyearly.*

Bisect, Dissect

Bisect means to divide into two equal or identical parts.
*The diagonals of a parallelogram **bisect** each other.*

Dissect means to cut apart and examine something.
*The students plan to **dissect** the preserved frog next week.*

Blackout, Brownout

Blackout is a total electrical power failure over a large area.
In 1965 and 1989, blackouts affected areas of New York.

Brownout is an interruption or temporary drop of electrical power.
A brownout caused my computer screen to flicker a few times.

Blatant, Flagrant

Blatant is an adjective meaning obvious.
We made a blatant mistake by overlooking Gary's contributions.

Flagrant means notoriously evil, bad, or objectionable.
The crew of the ship had an open and flagrant mutiny.

Bloc, Block

Bloc is a coalition of people, groups, or nations with a common goal.
Italy, France, and Spain formed a bloc to promote trade.

Use **block** for all other meanings.

Blond, Blonde

Blond refers to a boy or a man. **Blonde** refers to a girl or a woman.

Boar, Boor, Bore

Boar refers to a male pig.
After the 4-H Fair, Amy washed her prize-winning boar.

Boor refers to a crude, unrefined, or insensitive person.
He sometimes can be a loud, obnoxious boor during meetings.

Bore refers to being dull, tiresome, or tedious.
Reading was a bore until he discovered Harry Potter books.

Bona fide, Bonafied

Bona fide is the correct spelling.
I wouldn't consider his radio show a bona fide news program.

Boom to the economy, Boon to the economy

Boon to the economy, meaning a timely economic benefit or state, is the correct phrase.
*The new factory will be a **boon to the economy**.*

Born, Borne

Born means brought into life. It also is used to indicate one has a natural talent for something.
*His first son was **born** on Father's Day.*
*Bruce is so fast, people say he was **born** to run.*

Borne means to be carried or to endure something.
*Lyme disease is the most common tick-**borne** disease.*
*He has **borne** their mistakes with the patience of a saint.*

Bouillon, Bullion

Bouillon refers to clear, seasoned soup usually made from beef.
*The **bouillon** has no MSG and only one gram of fat per serving.*

Bullion refers to gold or silver.
*Brokers of **bullion** act as agents for buyers and sellers.*

Boycott, Embargo

Boycott is the refrain of business or social relations to show protest.
*The consumers are **boycotting** all the company's products.*

Embargo is a government prohibition on trade with another nation.
*In 1987, England imposed a trade **embargo** on Iran.*

Braise, Braze

Braise means to cook slowly under a covered container.
*The chef **braises** his vegetables in lemon juice and butter.*

Braze means to solder.
*The plumber needs to **braze** all the pipe fittings in the house.*

Bran new, Brand new

Brand new, an expression meaning new (think of a brand coming fresh out of the fire), is the correct phrase. It has nothing to do with the name of a product.
*They looked forward to moving into the **brand new** house.*

Breach, Breech

Breach is an infraction or violation of some kind.
*By leaving the job site, Bob is guilty of a **breach** of contract.*

Use **breech** for all other meanings, such as **breech** delivery.

Breadth, Breath, Breathe

Breadth refers to distance, width, or scope.
*Damian's success reflects the **breadth** of his experience.*

Breath is the noun and **breathe** is the verb.
*We typically take several **breaths** when we **breathe** heavily.*

Bridal, Bridle

Bridal refers to a marriage ceremony.
*The **bridal** party stayed at the reception until 2 a.m.*

Bridle refers to the harness on a horse or to horseback riding.
*Make sure the horse's **bridle** is not too tight but yet snug.*
*Though the **bridle** path is long and winding, it is still enjoyable.*

Bridle also refers to restraint or control.
*The players should **bridle** their appetites before exercising.*

Briefcase, Attaché

See entry for **Attaché, Briefcase**.

Bring, Take

Bring means to carry something toward some place.
*When you finish writing the plan, please **bring** it to my office.*

Take means to carry something away from some place.
*When I finish reviewing the plan, please **take** it to your office.*

British Isles, Great Britain, United Kingdom

The **British Isles** consists of the **United Kingdom** and its islands (Orkneys, Shetlands, and the Isle of Man). **Great Britain** consists of England, Scotland, and Wales. The **United Kingdom** consists of Great Britain and Northern Ireland.

Broach, Brooch

Broach means to open, introduce, or bring up something.
Do not broach that subject with the other team members.

Brooch refers to a pin or ornament with a clasp.
Donna wore an expensive brooch to her high school reunion.

Brochure, Leaflet, Pamphlet

A **brochure** is a small booklet usually not longer than 24 pages.
A **leaflet** is small printed item usually not longer than four pages.
A **pamphlet** is a stapled publication of fewer than 100 pages.

Broken, Busted

Prefer **broken**. **Busted** is considered a nonstandard word.
Scott suffered a broken leg during Monday's football practice.

Brother-in-laws, Brothers-in-law

Brothers-in-law is the correct phrase.

Build off of, Build on

Build on is the correct phrase.
Build on the successes you have attained this year.

Burglary, Robbery, Theft

Burglary means breaking into a building to steal something.
Burglaries plagued the new development.

Robbery is the taking of one's property by threat or force.
London's Great Train Robbery of 1963 involved 20 people.

Theft is the taking of one's property without threat or force.
Identity theft is a fast-growing crime in America.
(Note: *Larceny* is the legal term for theft or stealing.)

Buttocks, Buttox
Buttocks is the correct spelling.

By and large, By in large
By and large is the correct phrase.

By the fact that, In the fact that
By the fact that is the correct phrase.
*The truth was established just **by the fact that** his alibi did not hold up well.*

*The **burglar** was **robbed** as he ran from the bank.*

C

An unusual word should be shunned as a ship would shun a reef.
— Julius Caesar

Cache, Cachet, Cash

Cache is a hiding place.
*The bears found a **cache** of food belonging to some hunters.*

Cache also is small, fast computer memory that holds recently accessed data.
*Could the **cache** handle the extra memory requirements?*

Cachet refers to a mark of authenticity, prestige, or quality.
*The state courts have a **cachet** that the local courts lack.*

Cash is ready money.
*His wallet was fat with **cash** when he left the poker game.*

Calendar, Calender, Colander

Calendar is the correct spelling for a system of recording time. **Calender** is an old word that refers to a machine used in finishing paper and cloth. A **colander** is a perforated, bowl-shaped kitchen utensil for draining liquids and rinsing food.

Callous, Callus

Callous refers to having an unfeeling attitude.
*Perhaps you're being too **callous** about their situation.*

Callus refers to a thickening or hardening of the skin.
*The tight running shoes gave Austin a **callus** on his foot.*

Calvary, Cavalry

Calvary, with a capital C, is the place in Jerusalem where Christ died. **Cavalry** are soldiers mounted on horseback.

Can, Could, May, Might

Can and **could** refer to capability, though **could** often implies some doubt.
*Unlike our previous server, this one **can** support up to 50 users.*
*I suppose our old car **could** make the drive to California.*

May and **might** refer to permission or possibility.
*When time permits, you **may** start working on the project.*
*If everything goes as planned, you **may** finish the project early.*
*We **might** be able to go to the party after the game.*

Can not, Cannot

Cannot is always one word.

Cancel, Delay, Postpone

Cancel means to stop something with no intent to reschedule.
*After three years, Eric decided to **cancel** his subscription.*

Delay means to put off until further notice.
*The heavy rains could **delay** the game for several hours.*

Postpone means to cancel something with the intent to reschedule.
*I hope the committee does not **postpone** the test another week.*

Canter, Cantor

Canter refers to a horse's gait.
*The thoroughbred's **canter** is one of strength, agility, and grace.*

Cantor refers to a singer, usually in a house of worship.
*Expect Lori as one of the **cantors** for this weekend's service.*

Canvas, Canvass

Canvas is the cloth used in tents or sails, or what painters use.
*You can enlarge photos on **canvas** to look like paintings.*

Canvass is getting political support from voters.
*As usual, Rob opted to **canvass** in his own neighborhood first.*

Capacity, Ability
*See entry for **Ability, Capacity**.*

Capital, Capitol
Capital refers to money, property, uppercase letters, a form of punishment, architecture, or the location of a government seat. Examples: The **capital** gain tax, **capital** letters, **capital** punishment, the pillar's **capital,** or the **capital** of New York State is Albany.

Capitol refers to buildings in which a state or national government meets. (The *C* in **Capitol** is usually uppercase.) Examples: The **Capitol** in Albany, **Capitol** Hill.

Capitulate, Recapitulate
Capitulate means to surrender, come to terms, or acquiesce. *NATO forced the country to **capitulate** to its demands.*

Recapitulate means to sum up, review briefly, or repeat. *Let us **recapitulate** what we have learned these last two days.*

Carat, Caret, Carrot, Karat
Carat is a measurement (200 milligrams) for gemstones. *Ty bought an engagement ring with a 1.5–**carat** diamond.*

Caret is a proofreader's mark to indicate insertion. It's also used in math to indicate exponentiation. *Editors often insert many **carets** on a writer's first draft. If the **caret** is not in the formula, you will get a different answer.*

Carrot is the orange root that Bugs Bunny enjoys eating. ***Carrots** grow best when planted in spring.*

Karat is a measurement showing the ratio of pure gold to other materials in an alloy. The measurement uses a base of 24 units. Pure gold, which is 24/24ths gold, is called 24-karat gold. *All their 12-**karat** jewelry is on sale through next weekend.*

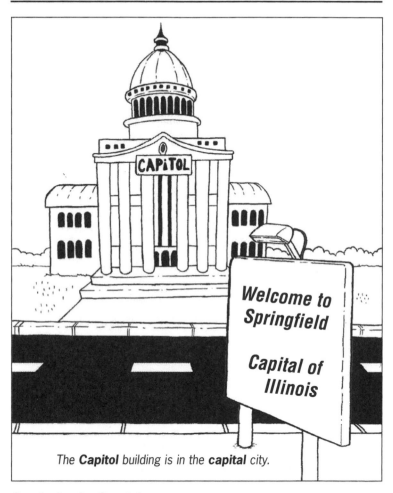

*The **Capitol** building is in the **capital** city.*

Card shark, Cardsharp

A **card shark** is a proficient, cutthroat, honest card player, and a **cardsharp** is a swindler.

Cardinal numbers, Ordinal numbers

Cardinal numbers (*1, five, 247*) refer to quantity but not order. *Despite all the traffic, we arrived **one** hour early for the concert.*

Ordinal numbers (*first, second, third,* and so on) refer to position or numerical sequence.
*Unlike in other years, this year our seats are in the **third** row.*

Careen, Career, Carom

Careen means to swerve or tilt while in motion.
*Despite improved suspension, the car **careened** during the race.*

Career means to move at full speed.
*The stock cars **careered** down the track.*

Carom means to collide and rebound.
*We held our breath as a few racing cars **caromed** off the wall.*

Carnivorous, Herbivorous, Omnivorous

Carnivorous refers to eating meat (or flesh).
*These **carnivorous** dinosaurs are from the Cretaceous period.*

Herbivorous refers to eating only plants.
*The iguanas and tortoises are typical **herbivorous** reptiles.*

Omnivorous refers to eating everything.
*An **omnivorous** diet consists of meats, fruits, grains, and vegetables.*

Case and point, Case in point

Case in point, meaning an example that supports a point, is the correct phrase.
*The low-carb diet works. I'm a **case in point**.*

Cease the day, Seize the day

Seize the day, which means to make the most of every moment, is the correct phrase.
*"**Seize the day**, put no trust in the morrow." – Horace.*

Cellar, Basement

See entry for **Basement, Cellar**.

Cement, Concrete

Cement is a powdery binding material that consists of clay and limestone. **Concrete** is a mixture of sand, gravel, and other materials all held together by **cement**.
*The workers are installing a **concrete** (not **cement**) sidewalk.*

Censor, Censure

Censor, as a verb, means to suppress objectionable material.
*Do they have a legal right to **censor** material on the Internet?*

Censor, as a noun, is the person examining the material.
*Are the TV **censors** approving the subject matter for broadcast?*

Censure means to blame, criticize strongly, or condemn.
*The principal **censured** the teacher for failing to stop the teasing.*

Centenarian, Centurion

A **centenarian** is a person who lives to be 100, and a **centurion** is a commander in the Roman army.

Center around

An impossibility. Use *center about, center in,* or *center on.*
*Today's Open House **centers on** the theme of Quality at Work.*

Ceremonial, Ceremonious

Ceremonial means being proper for a ceremony.
*She wore her traditional **ceremonial** dress to the banquet.*

Ceremonious means done in great ceremony (politely or formally).
*The new king offered a **ceremonious** toast at the gala.*

Cession, Session

Cession refers to an act of ceding (surrendering).
*It took the committee over two years to ratify the **cession** agreement.*

Session refers to a meeting or term.
*Scott is taking one course during the school's summer **session**.*

Chafe, Chaff

Chafe means to irritate or annoy something.
The new running shoes chafed John's feet.

Chaff, as a verb, means to tease good-naturedly.
Patty's teammates chaffed her for being late again to practice.

Chaff, as a noun, are husks separated from seeds during threshing.
The field workers literally separated the wheat from the chaff.

Chalked full, Chock full

Chock full, meaning completely full, is the correct phrase. Of naval origin, the saying comes from the phrase *chock-a-block*, which refers to two blocks of tackle stuck together so tightly they can't be tightened any further.
The technician recommended a web site chock full of useful tools.

Champ at the bit, Chomp at the bit

Champ at the bit is the correct phrase. The expression, which means eager or impatient, refers to an excited horse biting (*champing*) its bit. Because of constant misuse, *chomp at the bit* is becoming more common.
James champs at the bit when he sees the other soccer team take the field.

Chantey, Shanty

Chantey refers to a song sung by sailors while working.
As the crew washed the deck, the captain requested a chantey.

Shanty refers to a roughly built shack.
While stranded on the island, the crew lived in a small shanty.

Character, Reputation

Character refers to a person's personality.
His spontaneous reaction is completely out of character.

Reputation refers to the external perception of a person.
In spite of her reputation as fair, she was not a good umpire.

Cheap, Inexpensive

Cheap describes something that has a low price and is of low quality.
*We filled our first apartment with **cheap**, second-hand furniture.*

Inexpensive means low cost.
*The software was **inexpensive**, but did the job perfectly.*

Childish, Childlike

Childish means inappropriately acting like or resembling a child.
*The painting looks like **childish** scribble rather than creative art.*

Childlike means retaining some positive attributes of childhood.
*Even in his 60s, Ken retains a **childlike** love of rock music.*

Chord, Cord

Chord refers to a group of musical notes.
*Many of the group's earlier hits consisted of just three **chords**.*

Cord refers to a vocal cord, a cord of wood, or a rope.
*The high notes and fast tempo strained his vocal **cords**.*
*To be on the safe side, I bought two **cords** of wood for winter.*
*Please pull the **cord** when you get to the back door.*

Choreography, Chorography

Choreography refers to the art of dance design, and **chorography** refers to the art of map making.

Chronic, Acute

*See entry for **Acute, Chronic**.*

Cite, Sight, Site

Cite means to quote or mention something.
*When you write a term paper for Dr. Hards, **cite** your references.*

Sight is something seen, an ability to see, the foreseeable future, or an optical instrument.
*The ship's passengers soon caught **sight** of the beautiful island.*
*The passengers **sighted** the island from a mile out.*

*Unfortunately, there is no compromise or solution in **sight**.*
*Before target practice, John adjusts the **sight** on his rifle.*

Site refers to a location.
*The natural terrain lends itself to being a good **site** for a house.*

Citizen, Resident

A **citizen** is someone who has the full rights of a nation, either by birth or naturalization. A **resident** lives in a community but doesn't necessarily have the rights of a citizen.

Claim, Assert

*See entry for **Assert, Claim**.*

Classic, Classical

Classic refers to a long-established, usually high, standard.
*Babe Ruth had a **classic** baseball swing.*

Classical refers to the arts, literature, and architecture of ancient Greece and Rome. In music, **classical** means music from the 18th century European tradition, as opposed to pop or rock.
*Molly would rather play **classical** piano pieces.*

Cliché, Clique

Cliché is an overused expression.
*Good writers usually try to avoid using **clichés** in their writing.*

Clique refers to a small, exclusive group of people.
*To the dismay of some, many **cliques** exist in their high school.*

Click, Press, Type

Click means pressing and releasing the mouse button once.
*To start the program, **click** the red icon on the desktop.*

Press means to put force on something.
*If it fails again, **press** the Reset button on the computer once.*

Type means pressing a character key on a keyboard.
*After you have entered all the data, **type** the word EXIT.*

Climactic, Climatic

Climactic refers to the culmination of events (a climax).
The special effects in the climactic scene of the film are dull.

Climatic refers to meteorological conditions.
The Ice Age ushered in severe climatic conditions.

Climax, Acme

See entry for Acme, Climax.

Cohere, Adhere

See entry for Adhere, Cohere.

Collaborate, Corroborate

Collaborate means to aid, cooperate, or work together.
The churches collaborated on the holiday project for the needy.

Corroborate means to strengthen by confirming something.
The witness corroborated the defendant's testimony.

Collectable, Collectible

Either spelling is acceptable.

College, University

A **college** mainly grants bachelor's degrees. A **university** grants bachelor's, master's, and doctorate degrees.

Collision, Collusion

Collision refers to a crash.
The sudden collision of the two ships raises serious questions.

Collusion refers to a secret agreement between parties.
The high prices in winter could be the result of collusion among the companies.

Cologne, Perfume

Cologne is a weak, relatively inexpensive fragrance. **Perfume** is a strong, relatively expensive fragrance.

Comedian, Comedienne

Comedian refers to a male comic, and **comedienne** refers to a female comic.

Common, Mutual, Ordinary, Popular

Common means widespread or prevalent.
*That type of mosquito is a **common** disease carrier.*

Mutual means shared by two or more parties.
***Mutual** trust is a key ingredient for a long-term relationship.*

Ordinary means plain or undistinguished.
*Her high grades reflect study habits that are far from **ordinary**.*

Popular means liked or preferred by the masses.
*The **popular** game is played by children everywhere.*

Compare and Contrast

A redundancy. When you **compare** things, you note both differences and similarities. When you **contrast** things, you note just the differences. Therefore, use **compare** or **contrast** separately but not together.

Compare to, Compare with

Compare to and **compare with** often are used interchangeably, but **compare to** can mean liken, while **compare with** always means differences are being examined.
*The author and entertainer **compared** his world **to** a stage.*
***Compared with** 1996, the 2000 election was problematic.*

Complacent, Complaisant

Complacent refers to a feeling of self-satisfaction, to the point that one becomes lazy.
*After much success, the film director grew **complacent**.*

Complaisant refers to a willingness to comply or oblige.
*An energetic and **complaisant** guide gave us a tour of campus.*

Complement

Complement, Compliment

Complement, as a noun, is a group that completes a set.
*A **complement** of four people would now bring the staff to nine.*

Complement, as a verb, means to go well with something.
*The four new people would **complement** the rest of the staff.*

Compliment, as a noun, is an expression of courtesy or praise.
*The supervisor gave the staff a **compliment** on its work.*

Compliment, as a verb, means to praise or respect something.
*The supervisor regularly **compliments** the staff on its work.*

Compose, Comprise

Compose means to create or to make up the whole.
*John Williams **composes** musical scores for Spielberg films.*
*Five thousand songs **compose** the college's new music library.*

Comprise means to consist of something.
*The college's new music library **comprises** 5,000 songs.*

Memory hook: The whole **comprises** the parts, and the parts **compose** the whole.

Comprehensible, Comprehensive

Comprehensible means understandable or intelligible.
*Despite all the technical jargon, the book is **comprehensible**.*

Comprehensive means comprising many things or large in scope.
*Jim did a **comprehensive** study on Internet sales.*

Comptroller, Controller

Comptroller is a variant spelling for **controller**. Both words refer to the chief accountant in an organization. **Comptroller** is usually used in government-related positions, and **controller** is more common in private industry.

Compulsion, Compunction

Compulsion refers to a forced impulse, compliance, or drive.
*Lennon had a **compulsion** to make the Beatles a top rock band.*

Compunction refers to remorse or regret for one's actions.
*He showed much **compunction** about leaving his old job.*

Compulsive, Compulsory, Impulsive

Compulsive refers to feeling compelled about something.
*Tom **compulsively** cleans his car.*

Compulsory refers to being obligated to do something.
*Les took a **compulsory** physical examination for his new job.*

Impulsive refers to doing things on the spur of the moment.
*Occasionally Ed gets **impulsive** and buys expensive wine.*

Concede, Accede, Exceed

*See entry for **Accede, Concede, Exceed**.*

Concert, Recital

Concert refers to a performance given by two or more people.
*The Beatles last American **concert** was in 1966.*

Recital refers to a performance given by one person (a soloist).
*Her Christmas piano **recital** went better than anyone expected.*

Concurrent, Consecutive

Concurrent means simultaneous or happening at the same time.
*Management held **concurrent** meetings at all of the company's locations to announce the reorganization.*

Consecutive means successive or following one after the other.
*The pitcher threw six **consecutive** strikes during the last inning.*

Conducive to, Conducive with

Conducive to is the preferred phrase.
*Good working conditions can be **conducive to** productivity.*

Confectionary, Confectionery

Confectionary is the place where you buy confections, and **confectionery** is a sweet such as candy or ice cream.

Confidant, Confident

Confidant refers to a trustworthy friend.
*Sue is her **confidant** as well as her legal advisor.*

Confident refers to being self assured.
*Liam is **confident** that his unique house design will be sold.*

Congenial, Congenital, Genial

Congenial means having the same nature, disposition, or tastes.
*We work in a **congenial** atmosphere that all of us enjoy.*

Congenital means existing in an individual since birth.
*His health problems can be traced to a rare **congenital** disorder.*

Genial means agreeable, pleasing, or compatible.
*The retirees are traveling and enjoying Hawaii's **genial** climate.*

Connote, Denote

Connote means to imply or suggest something.
*His actions **connote** he is unhappy living there.*

Denote means to indicate or refer to specifically.
*We were just taught the symbol for pi **denotes** the number 3.14159.*

Note: **Connote** and **denote** are preferable to *connotate* and *denotate*. Both of these words are considered obsolete.

Conscience, Conscious

Conscience means a sense of right and wrong.
*His **conscience** didn't bother him when he fired his friend.*

Conscious means to be aware of something or to be awake.
*Sue made a **conscious** decision to practice her piano lessons daily.*
*Though he hit his head, he was **conscious** after the accident.*

Consequent, Subsequent

Consequent means following as a direct result.
*Jan's excellent evaluation and **consequent** pay raise made her day.*

Subsequent means occurring after.
__Subsequent__ to the installation, my desktop icons would not load.

Consistently, Constantly

Consistently means steadfast, unwavering, or without change.
*Airline tickets **consistently** rank among the most popular Internet items.*

Constantly means unceasing, perpetual, or without interruption.
*In a **constantly** changing technical world, training is essential.*

Consul, Council, Counsel

Consul is an official representing one's country in another country.
*A new **consul** was appointed last week for the Republic of Chad.*

Council is a group appointed or elected to make decisions.
*Most cities and towns have a **council** that governs certain areas.*

Counsel, as a noun, is an attorney; as a verb, it means to give advice.
*His **counsel** (attorney) did an excellent job of building a case.*
*The social worker tried unsuccessfully to **counsel** the parents.*

Contagious, Infectious

Contagious refers to diseases spread through physical contact.
*If you deal with **contagious** diseases, disinfect your hands well.*

Infectious refers to diseases spread through air, water, etc.
*We are exposed to chemicals and **infectious** diseases.*

Note: In figurative use, these words can be synonymous.
*Her optimistic and humorous mood is **infectious** (or **contagious**).*

*The **counsel** told the **consul** what to say to the city **council**.*

Contemptible, Contemptuous

Contemptible means worthy of contempt or deserving scorn.
*The board thinks Keith's treatment of the intern is **contemptible**.*

Contemptuous means expressing a feeling of contempt.
*They risk disciplinary action for making **contemptuous** remarks.*

Contentious, Controversial

Contentious means argumentative or quarrelsome.
*The measure was defeated after a **contentious** House debate.*

Controversial refers to subjects being arguable or debatable.
*They extended the deadline on the **controversial** change.*

Conterminous, Contiguous

Conterminous means contained within one boundary.
The conterminous United States excludes two states: Alaska and Hawaii.

Contiguous means sharing a boundary or touching.
The suburb of Oak Park is contiguous with Chicago.

Continual, Continuous

Continual means repeatedly, but not necessarily without interruptions.
Jane continually ignores her boss' requests for more coffee.

Continuous means constantly or without interruptions.
The border runs continuously from the river to the mountains.

Continuance, Continuation

Continuance refers to the duration of a state or condition.
Her continuance in office depends on the November election.

Continuation refers to the resumption of something.
Today's meeting is just a continuation of yesterday's meeting.

Contrary, Converse

To be **contrary** means to differ or disagree with something.
Contrary to belief, Joe was a good football coach.

Converse means the opposite of something.
We held the converse view that the executive was effective.

Convert into, Convert to

Convert into means to change from one thing to another.
The tool converts PDF documents into HTML or ASCII text.

Convert to means to switch allegiance, loyalty, or obligation.
While attending college, John converted to another faith.

Convince, Persuade

Convince means causing someone to believe through evidence. *His minty breath **convinced** the teacher that Fred had brushed his teeth.*

Persuade means causing someone to act through reasoning. *The class **persuaded** Diane to run for re-election in the spring.*

Copyright, Copywrite

Copyright is the correct word.

Core, Corps

Core refers to a central or essential part. *A **core** rule of their company is a strict dress code.*

Corps refers to people acting as a body rather than individuals. *He and a few other people we know belong to the Peace **Corps**.*

Corespondent, Correspondent

Corespondent is a person charged with adultery in a divorce suit. *The **corespondent** never admitted to an affair with the woman.*

Correspondent is a communicator, such as a writer. *Kathy worked as a special **correspondent** for the network.*

Cornet, Coronet

A **cornet** is the musical instrument. A **coronet** is a small crown or headband, or the upper margin of a horse's hoof.

Corrode, Erode

Corrode means to be eaten away by a chemical reaction. *The rust will immediately **corrode** the brass if it is not removed.*

Erode means to wear away by water or wind. *The heavy spring rains **eroded** the high cliffs by their house.*

Note: Both of these words can also be used figuratively. *Mistrust can **corrode** any good business partnership. Confidence in their leadership **eroded** over the years.*

Could care less, Could not care less
Though it is a cliché, **could not care less** is the correct phrase.
He could not care less about learning how to play bridge.

Could have, Could of
Could have is the correct phrase.
During last night's meeting, you could have heard a pin drop.

Councilor, Counselor
A **councilor** serves on a council and a **counselor** offers counsel and advice.

Country, Nation
A **country** is a piece of land or area and the home of certain people. A **nation** is a body of people associated with a particular area or territory.

Coup de grace, Coup de gras
Coup de grace, meaning a decisive event, is the correct phrase.
If they are defeated today, it could be their coup de grace.

Covert, Overt
Covert means concealed, covered, or hidden.
Mike's company provides covert video surveillance equipment.

Overt means open to view, plain, apparent, or public.
England continues to offer the United States its overt support.

Cramp my style, Crimp my style
Cramp my style is the correct phrase.

Cream de mint, Crème de menthe
Crème de menthe is the correct phrase.

Credible, Creditable, Credulous
Credible means believable.
Though it's a strange and unusual story, it seems credible.

Creditable means worthy of praise or credit.
*The band gave a **creditable** performance in Syracuse.*

Credulous means gullible.
*Even a **credulous** fan doesn't believe seats are still available.*

Crevasse, Crevice

Crevasse is a deep opening or crack usually found in a glacier.
*Fran is standing too close to the **crevasse** of the glacier.*

Crevice is a narrow opening or crack in a wall, floor, or rock.
*A bat can find the smallest **crevice** to sleep in during the day.*

Criteria, Criterion

Criteria is the plural form; **criterion** is the singular form.
*They identified 10 important **criteria** for their business plan.*
*The most important **criterion** for us is customer acceptance.*

Note: Phrases such as *a criteria, one criteria,* or *this criteria* should be avoided. Also, a few writing authorities accept *criterions* as the plural of **criterion**.

Criticize, Critique

Critique (noun or verb) means a critical review of something.
*The professor's **critique** of the film annoyed some people.*
*Professor Ward **critiques** movies for the Binghamton Press.*

Criticize means to offer critical remarks about something.
*Tim **criticized** Walter for his indifference to politics.*

Croquet, Croquette

Croquet is a lawn game using mallets, balls, and wickets.
*Historians think **croquet** began as an outdoor version of billiards.*

Croquette is a small cake of minced food usually coated in bread crumbs and deep fried.
*Beef stock, spices, potatoes, and meat made up the filling of the **croquette**.*

Cue, Queue

Cue refers to a signal to begin something.
*The actors are getting their **cues** from the orchestra conductor.*

Queue refers to people or things in line.
*Is that your document or someone else's in the print **queue**?*

Curtains, Draperies

Curtains are smaller, less fancy, and typically easier to hang than **draperies**.

Cut and dried, Cut and dry

Cut and dried, which means finished, is the correct expression. The phrase comes from the timber industry, and refers to an area that has been cut clear of trees (clear cut).
*The supervisor's plans are not as **cut and dried** as you think.*

Cynical, Sarcastic, Skeptical

Cynical means contemptuously distrustful of someone's motives.
*"Those **cynical** men who say that democracy cannot be honest and efficient." –* Franklin D. Roosevelt

Sarcastic means using bitter or caustic language against someone.
*The **sarcastic** clerk cost the store many customers.*

Skeptical means doubting, questioning, or mistrustful.
*Candy seemed **skeptical** when I told her I am seeing a psychic.*

Cynosure, Sinecure

Cynosure refers to something that strongly attracts attention.
*"Where perhaps some beauty lies, the **cynosure** of neighboring eyes." –* Milton

Sinecure refers to a position or office that requires little or no responsibilities.
*"A lucrative **sinecure** in the Excise." –* Macaulay

D

A word in earnest is as good as a speech. – Charles Dickens

Damage, Damages

Damage refers to destruction of some kind.
The sun's UVA and UVB rays can permanently damage the skin.

Damages refer to compensation awarded by a court of law.
The court awarded substantial damages to the affected families.

Dare say, Daresay

Either spelling is acceptable.

Data, Datum

Data is the plural of **datum**.
The Census Bureau collects these data from each agency.

Note: In technical writing, **data** (as a collective noun) often takes a singular verb.
The online numeric data is restricted to privileged users.

Daughter-in-laws, Daughters-in-law

Daughters-in-law is the correct phrase.

Daylight saving time, Daylight savings time

Daylight saving time is the correct phrase.

Deadly, Deathly

Deadly means likely to cause death.
Research shows aspirin can reduce the risk of deadly infections.

Deathly means like or in the manner of death.
After the loss, a deathly silence fell across the stadium.

Dearth, Plethora

Dearth refers to a great shortage or scarcity of something.
We have a dearth of competent workers to handle the project.

Plethora refers to an abundance or excess of something.
The holiday season brings a plethora of "Greatest Hits" CDs.

Debar, Disbar

Debar means to bar from a place or to prevent from exercising a right.
Many states debar people under 21 from alcohol and tobacco.

Disbar means to expel from the bar or the legal profession.
He avoided prosecution, but they may still disbar him.

Debark, Disembark

Both words mean to go ashore or to unload something. Either is acceptable.

Decent, Descent, Dissent

Decent means proper or honest.
The play's interpretation was done in a decent manner.
Many people consider Rick a thoughtful and decent individual.

Descent means a downward slope or family origin.
The airplane's sudden descent alarmed many of the passengers.
When one mentions the descent of man, we think of Darwin.

Dissent means disagreement.
If the cause made real sense, there would not be much dissent.

Decided, Decisive, Incisive

Decided means clear-cut, unmistakable, or without doubt.
This company has a decided advantage over its competitors.

Decisive means conclusive.
The committee's decisive action gave our firm an advantage.

Incisive means acute, cutting, or sharp.
The company lost an incisive mind and an outstanding engineer.

Decimate

Decimate, Annihilate
*See entry for **Annihilate, Decimate**.*

Decry, Descry
Decry means to openly condemn or ridicule something.
*The faculty has a right to **decry** the cuts in the budget.*

Descry means to see or catch sight of, often from a distance.
*Some nights you can actually **descry** the blue whales out at sea.*

Deduce, Deduct, Adduce
*See entry for **Adduce, Deduce, Deduct**.*

Deductive, Inductive
Concerning types of reasoning:

Deductive means to reason from the general to the specific (top-down approach).
Example: *All people need water to survive; Bob is a person; Bob needs water to survive.*

Inductive means to reason from the specific to the general (bottom-up approach).
Example: *Bob needs water to survive; Bob is a person; all people need water to survive.*

De facto, De jure
De facto means actual.
*The **de facto** speed limit on a busy afternoon is only 50 m.p.h.*

De jure means as a matter of law or right.
*The maximum speed limit, **de jure**, is 65 m.p.h.*

Defective, Deficient
Defective means faulty.
*The scanner's **defective** circuit board can easily be replaced.*

Deficient means lacking completeness or a key ingredient.
*Tests proved her diet was **deficient** in calcium and magnesium.*

Deference, Difference, Diffidence

Deference means courteous regard or respect.
*The young reporter showed **deference** to the famous anchor.*

Difference means a distinguishing characteristic or disparity.
*The **difference** is in how they present themselves to the public.*

Diffidence means reserved, shy, or lacking self confidence.
*Overcoming their **diffidence** may lead to better opportunities.*

Definite, Definitive

Definite means certain, precise, explicit, or clear.
*After the game, I had a **definite** feeling of accomplishment.*

Definitive means final, decisive, and authoritative.
*The interested party immediately gave us a **definitive** answer.*

Defuse, Diffuse

Defuse means to remove a fuse (usually from an explosive).
*The company hired an explosives expert to **defuse** the bomb.*

Diffuse means to spread out.
*The mouse's odor **diffused** throughout the entire house.*

Delay, Cancel, Postpone

*See entry for **Cancel, Delay, Postpone**.*

Delegate, Relegate

Delegate means to assign others to a task.
*The officials may **delegate** authority to the appropriate people.*

Relegate means send or consign to an obscure place or position.
*After I fell, I was **relegated** to a backup spot on the team.*

Deluge, Flood

A **deluge** is a large, heavy downpour of water that typically does not leave damage. A **flood** is overflowing water that covers land. It typically leaves damage.

Delusion

Delusion, Allusion, Illusion

See entry for **Allusion, Delusion, Illusion**.

Demur, Demure

Demur means to voice opposition, objection, or delay.
Jim may **demur** *at the suggestion that we start the meeting now.*

Demure means modest, reserved, or shy.
Peter appears **demure** *despite all of his accomplishments.*

Denote, Connote

See entry for **Connote, Denote**.

Denounce, Renounce

Denounce means to criticize or condemn something openly.
The new drug was **denounced** *as ineffective and harmful.*

Renounce means to give up claim to something.
The engineer willingly **renounced** *all ownership to the software.*

Depraved, Deprived

Depraved means morally bad or corrupt.
A **depraved** *person can have a bad influence on other people.*

Deprived means lacking economic or social necessities.
We distributed the food baskets to **deprived** *neighborhoods.*

Deprecate, Depreciate

Deprecate means to disapprove of or belittle something.
Tom **deprecated** *his contributions to the company's success.*

Depreciate means to lower the value or worth of something.
Years of city driving drastically **depreciated** *the value of my car.*

Descension, Dissension

Descension means to descend, fall, or sink.
The team's sudden **descension** *in the rankings surprised many.*

Dissension means disagreement or a difference of opinion.
Dissension *exists over where the new town hall should be built.*

Desert, Dessert

Desert, as a noun, is an arid place with little vegetation, or something deserved or merited, especially a punishment.
*The **desert** ranges of the Southwest are beautiful places to visit.*
*When the old plan was revealed, they received their just **deserts**.*

Desert, as a verb, means to abandon or forsake.
*Despite financial setbacks, he refuses to **desert** the company.*

Dessert, the noun, is the sweet thing one eats at the end of a meal.
*After dinner, we usually stop at the bakery for **dessert**.*

Desolate, Dissolute

Desolate means uninhabited or miserable.
*Chris and Bill decided to retire in a **desolate** part of Maine.*
*The children are **desolate** over the loss of their dog last year.*

Dissolute means lacking in moral standards.
*I regret having lived a **dissolute** lifestyle in my younger years.*

Despatch, Dispatch

Dispatch is preferred in American usage.

Desperate, Disparate

Desperate means nearly hopeless or undertaken as a last resort.
*We are taking **desperate** measures to avoid another strike.*

Disparate means completely distinct or different.
*The candidates' ideas reflect **disparate** visions of government's role.*

Despise, Hate

Despise means to regard with contempt or to look down on.
*It's their successful economy that is so **despised** by the group.*

Hate means to dislike intensely or to loathe something.
*It seems people either love or **hate** mayonnaise on sandwiches.*

Detract, Distract

Detract means to take away a part or to lessen something.
*Their odd behavior **detracts** from their accomplishments.*

Distract means to divert, confound, or harass something.
*The noise in the balcony **distracted** her attention from the play.*

Device, Devise

Device refers to a gadget.
*In addition to the PC, the personal copier is a useful **device**.*

Devise means to think of something.
*The President and his staff **devised** a plan to help the economy.*

Dexterous, Dextrous

Though **dexterous** is more common, either spelling is correct.

Diagnosis, Prognosis

Diagnosis is the identification of a problem, most commonly a medical condition.
*The **diagnosis** is a slight tear in the right knee's cartilage.*

Prognosis is a forecast or prediction.
*The doctor offered his **prognosis** that knee surgery would help.*

Dialate, Dilate

Dilate is the correct word.

Dialectal, Dialectical

Dialectal refers to a dialect or a regional language.
*Nine major **dialectal** regions exist in China.*

Dialectical refers to a method for arriving at the truth.
*Some philosophers use the Socratic **dialectical** method of cross-examination.*

Dialog, Dialogue
Though **dialogue** is more common, either spelling is acceptable.

Differ from, Differ with
Differ from means to differ between one person or thing and another.
*My car **differs from** Joe's in that it is equipped with a CB radio.*

Differ with means to differ in opinion (disagree).
*I **differed with** her opinion of the new high school principal.*

Different from, Different than
Different from is used when comparing items.
*Excluding cost, her car is **different from** mine in many ways.*

Different than is used when a subject and verb (a clause) follow the phrase.
*Her job today is much **different than** it was five years ago.*

Dilemma, Problem
Dilemma is a situation that requires a choice between undesirable options.
*The chairperson is caught in a **dilemma** between lying and admitting he embezzled the money.*

Problem is a situation, matter, or person that presents perplexity or difficulty.
*They have a **problem** with the supervisor's leadership.*

Diminish, Minimize
Diminish means to reduce, shrink, or make less important.
*Glycolic acid can help **diminish** facial lines and wrinkles.*

Minimize means to reduce to the smallest degree or size.
*Exercises to the stomach muscles can **minimize** back pain.*

Diplomat, Diplomate

Diplomat is one skilled in negotiations, good manners, and tact.
*The **diplomat** offered an effective resolution to the conflict.*

Diplomate is a physician certified as a specialist by a medical board.
*Dr. Walker is a **diplomate** of the American Board of Plastic Surgery.*

Disapprove, Disprove

Disapprove means to withhold approval of something.
*Do you **disapprove** of the way Lou is handling his job?*

Disprove means to prove the falsity of something.
*Even if you **disprove** Jim's claim, he may file again.*

Disassemble, Dissemble

Disassemble means to take something apart.
*To **disassemble** the hardware, follow the instructions.*

Dissemble means to disguise or conceal behind a false appearance.
*The man attempted to **dissemble** his guilt with laughter.*

Disassociate, Dissociate

Either spelling is acceptable, though **dissociate** is preferred.

Disburse, Disperse

Disburse means to pay out or expend.
*Accounting should **disburse** the travel compensation next week.*

Disperse means to scatter something.
*The road crew will **disperse** the road salt before rush hour.*

Discomfit, Discomfort

Discomfit means to frustrate, disconcert, or baffle.
*Their questionable comments may **discomfit** the employees.*

Discomfort means pain, uneasiness, or distress.
*Helen's sprained wrist gave her **discomfort** during the match.*

Discover, Invent

Discover means to find something already in existence, but unknown.
*While on the expedition, Pete **discovered** a few new species.*

Invent means to create something new.
*Edison **invented** many useful devices for society.*

Discovered Missing

This is a contradiction. Just say **missing**.

*The men **dispersed** as soon as the pay was **disbursed**.*

Discreet, Discrete

Discreet means to be careful about what one does or says.
*If you ask for a raise, be **discreet**; I don't want Jim to know.*

Discrete means separate or distinct.
*The conversion process consists of five **discrete** steps.*

Discrepancy, Disparity

Discrepancy is a difference between facts or claims.
*The appraised value and the asking price show a **discrepancy**.*

Disparity means inequality or incongruity.
*We found a big **disparity** between their ideals and their actions.*

Discriminate, Distinguish

Discriminate means to perceive differences and use that perception to make a judgment.
*The players could not **discriminate** between a good golf hole and a bad one.*

Distinguish means to recognize qualities or features of a thing that make it different from others.
*The groundskeeper could easily **distinguish** bent grass from Kentucky blue grass.*

Disenfranchise, Disfranchise

Disfranchise is preferred in American usage.

Disinformation, Misinformation

Disinformation refers to deliberately misleading information.
*The competition gave us **disinformation** about their products.*

Misinformation refers to incorrect information.
*The paper printed **misinformation** about the concert dates.*

Disingenuous, Ingenious, Ingenuous

Disingenuous means devious, dishonest, or pretending.
*He's being rather **disingenuous**, saying the computer runs well.*

Ingenious means clever, imaginative, or original.
*Art developed an **ingenious** solution to the hardware problem.*

Ingenuous means candid, honest, or innocent.
*Jill and Rick have an open, **ingenuous** manner that people like.*

Disinterested, Uninterested

Disinterested means impartial, neutral, objective, or unbiased.
*We chose Maria as a **disinterested** third party to decide our fate.*

Uninterested means bored, indifferent, or simply not interested.
*Despite Tom's elaborate proposal, his boss remains obviously **uninterested** in the project.*

Disorganized, Unorganized

Disorganized means thrown into disorder or disarray.
*We have never seen a dormitory room so **disorganized**!*

Unorganized means not yet organized or lacking order.
*Though the league started last year, it still appears **unorganized**.*

Disorientated, Disoriented

Disoriented, meaning to feel displaced, is the preferred spelling.
*Lori felt groggy and **disoriented** after her long flight.*

Disparage, Disparate

Disparage means to criticize or belittle someone.
*His comment was not meant to **disparage** a nice guy like Ed.*

Disparate means different or distinct in quality or kind.
*The local charity event brought many **disparate** people together.*

Dispense with, Dispose of

Dispense with means to do without something.
*We would like to **dispense with** all the unnecessary paperwork.*

Dispose of means to get rid of something.
*Where can I properly **dispose of** the used oil and paint thinner?*

Displace

Displace, Misplace

Displace means to shift, change, or move.
Last summer the raging floods displaced many residents.

Misplace means to lose something or put it in the wrong place.
It's easy to misplace a punctuation mark in a complex sentence.

Dissatisfied, Unsatisfied

Dissatisfied means not satisfied, and has a critical connotation.
They were dissatisfied with the food and service at the diner.

Unsatisfied also means not satisfied, but doesn't necessarily imply criticism.
His hunger was unsatisfied despite the large meal he ate.

Dissect, Bisect

*See entry for **Bisect, Dissect**.*

Distinct, Distinctive

Distinct means clearly apparent, discrete, separate, or obvious.
A distinct improvement in giving helped many families last year.

Distinctive means distinguished or standing out as different.
J. Hayward's distinctive voice has won the band many fans.

Distraught, Diswraught

Distraught is the correct word.

Diversity, Adversity

*See entry for **Adversity, Diversity**.*

Divert, Avert, Avoid

*See entry for **Avert, Avoid, Divert**.*

Doctor, Physician

Doctor refers to anyone who has been granted a doctor's degree. **Physician** is a general term for a doctor of medicine, someone legally qualified to practice medicine. All physicians are doctors of medicine, but not all doctors practice medicine.

Doggy dog world, Dog-eat-dog world

Dog-eat-dog world is the correct phrase. It means that the world is ruthlessly competitive, and derives from a 16th century proverb that people may revert to the animal laws of survival. *With shrinking markets, it's now a **dog-eat-dog world** for many companies.*

Dogmatic, Pragmatic

Dogmatic means arrogantly authoritative or overbearing.
*His **dogmatic** and demanding personality did not fit in well here.*

Pragmatic means practical.
*Pat takes a **pragmatic** approach to teaching children.*

Dominant, Dominate, Domineer

Dominant means commanding or controlling over all others.
*The largest wolf is usually **dominant** in the pack.*

Dominate means to control, govern, or regulate something.
*Their software **dominates** the financial services industry.*

Domineer means to exercise arbitrary or overbearing control.
*The strong will of a few can sometimes **domineer** a community.*

Dosage, Dose

Dosage refers to a regimen of something and **dose** refers to a specific amount.
*Patients received an initial **dose** of 20 mg and thereafter a **dosage** of 10 mg twice a day for a month.*

Dough, Batter

*See entry for **Batter, Dough**.*

Douse, Dowse

Douse means to extinguish or wet thoroughly.
*The firefighters **doused** the flames with water most of the night.*

Dowse means to look for water or minerals with a divining rod.
*It was common for the pioneers to **dowse** for water on the trail.*

Down the pike, Down the pipe

Down the pike is the correct phrase. It means something is going to happen. The Pike was originally an elongated entertainment area at the 1904 St. Louis World's Fair. Fair goers would commonly say, *There's always something new coming down the Pike.*

Downfall, Drawback

Downfall refers to the destruction of something.
The Russian Revolution led to Czar Nicholas II's **downfall**.

Drawback refers to a flaw or problem of some kind.
Their plan to camp there had one **drawback**: *too many gnats.*

Downward, Downwards

Downward is preferred in American usage.

Draperies, Curtains

See entry for **Curtains, Draperies**.

Drowned, Drownded

Drowned is the correct word.

Dual, Duel

Dual refers to something in a pair.
After you install the **dual** *carburetors, open the throttle half way.*

Duel refers to a formal battle or contest intended to settle a dispute.
*"**Duel** of the Titans" is a film about Romulus and Remus.*

Duck tape, Duct tape

Duct tape is the correct phrase.
We told them to use **duct tape** *to seal the doors and windows.*

Due to, Because of

See entry for **Because of, Due to**.

E

Every word was once a poem.   – Ralph Waldo Emerson

E-Business, E-Commerce
E-Business refers to conducting general business on the Internet. **E-Commerce** refers specifically to the buying and selling of goods and services on the Internet.

Each other, One another
Each other refers to two persons or things.
*The interior and exterior colors complement **each other**.*

One another refers to more than two persons or things.
*Videoconferencing allows the diplomats to see **one another**.*

Eager, Anxious
See entry for **Anxious, Eager**.

Earthen, Earthly, Earthy
Earthen refers to being made of earth.
*Over the fire hangs a big **earthen** pot, the kind Indians used.*

Earthly refers to being of this world.
*Per his last request, his **earthly** remains were scattered at sea.*

Earthy refers to being down to earth, crude, or unrefined.
*The speaker's **earthy** expressions pleased the rebellious crowd.*

Eastward, Eastwards
Eastward is preferred in American usage.

Eclectic, Esoteric, Exoteric

Eclectic means the best of something from many sources. *With music from Bach to the Beatles, the show was clearly eclectic.*

Esoteric means confined to or understood by just a few people. *The author's use of esoteric language can deter the reader.*

Exoteric means suitable for all. *She designs and writes books for an exoteric audience.*

Ecology, Environment

Ecology refers to relationships between organisms and their environment. *Last semester the class studied the ecology of the jungle.*

Environment refers to conditions that surround an organism. *Many fear that nuclear waste can hurt our environment.*

Economic, Economical

Economic refers to the economy, material wealth, or financial reward. *They predict a substantial economic recovery for next year. We sold our Florida vacation house for economic reasons.*

Economical refers to being not wasteful. *This car is more economical on gas than the others we tried.*

Edition, Addition

See entry for Addition, Edition.

Eerie, Aerie, Airy

See entry for Aerie, Airy, Eerie.

Effect, Affect

See entry for Affect, Effect.

Effective, Effectual, Efficacious, Efficient

Effective means impressive, in effect, or producing a result.
*The band put on an **effective** performance at Saratoga.*
*The new fiscal calendar is **effective** as of next month.*
*The talks were **effective** in gaining peace within a few days.*

Effectual, like **effective**, means sufficient to produce a desired effect or result.
*"**Effectual** steps for the suppression of the rebellion."* - Macaulay

Efficacious means having the power to achieve the desired effect.
*The doctor discovered an **efficacious** remedy for the ailment.*

Efficient means achieving results through a good use of resources.
*Some fuel-**efficient** cars can get 60 miles to a gallon of gas.*

Effluent, Affluent
*See entry for **Affluent, Effluent**.*

Egression, Aggression
*See entry for **Aggression, Egression**.*

Either, Neither

Either means one or the other of two.
*It's **either** higher taxes or some cutbacks.*

Neither means not one nor the other of two.
*Under the new agreement, **neither** party may transfer its rights.*

Elapse, Lapse

Elapse means to pass by or slip away.
*How much time **elapses** before the officials make a decision?*

Lapse means to drift or discontinue.
*The magazine subscription **lapses** unless you renew it soon.*

Elegy, Eulogy

Elegy refers to a poem of lament or praise for a dead person.
*Walt Whitman wrote a famous **elegy** on the death of Lincoln.*

Eulogy refers to speech or writing in praise of someone, usually dead.
*Earl Spencer wrote a moving **eulogy** to his sister, Princess Diana.*

Elicit, Illegal, Illicit

Elicit means to bring out or draw forth.
*The band's performances always **elicit** praise from the critics.*

Illegal means unlawful.
*It is **illegal** to use a handheld cell phone while driving.*

Illicit means unlawful or prohibited.
*The council fined the firm because of its **illicit** activities.*

Elude, Allude, Refer

*See entry for **Allude, Elude, Refer**.*

Elusive, Illusive

Elusive means hard to catch, grasp, or define.
*Director Stanley Kubrick remained an **elusive** figure to the press.*

Illusive means deceptive or unreal.
*David Copperfield amazes audiences with **illusive** magic tricks.*

Embargo, Boycott

*See entry for **Boycott, Embargo**.*

Emend, Amend

*See entry for **Amend, Emend**.*

Emerge, Immerge, Immerse

Emerge means to come out, rise up, or come forth.
*More vacation time may **emerge** from the contract talks.*

Immerge and **immerse** mean to plunge into or submerge.
Immerge (immerse) the knee in ice to minimize the swelling.

Emigrant, Immigrant, Migrant

Emigrant is one who leaves one's country to settle in another.
The emigrants spent a few weeks aboard ship before landing.

Immigrant is one who enters and settles in a new country.
Many immigrants are looking for jobs in the metropolitan area.

Migrant is one who travels about, especially in search of work.
The migrants are working in the apple orchards of New York.

Eminent, Immanent, Imminent

Eminent means distinguished, famous, or prominent.
Eminent scientists have serious concerns about the coral reefs.

Immanent means inherent or present within the universe.
The theologian suggests that God is immanent in all life forms.

Imminent means about to happen or threatening.
The bidders tell us the government contract award is imminent.

Emollient, Emolument

Emollient refers to a softening, soothing, or less harsh effect.
He took a more emollient approach than his harsh predecessor.

Emolument refers to salary, wages, or perquisites.
The emolument rate for late-night work will be increased.

Empathy, Sympathy

Empathy is the ability to relate to someone.
Having been poor as a child, Harry Chapin always had empathy for the hungry.

Sympathy means feeling sorry for someone.
The club conveyed its sympathy to the widow with a gift basket.

Empirical, Imperial

Empirical means verifiable or provable by means of observation or experiment.
No empirical evidence exists to suggest the accused was anywhere near the crime.

Emulate

Imperial means relating to or suggestive of an empire or a sovereign.
*Unfortunately, they acted on their **imperial** impulses and invaded the small country.*

Emulate, Simulate

Emulate means strive to equal or excel, usually through imitation.
*The new TV comedy tried to **emulate** Seinfeld.*

Simulate means to take on the appearance of something.
*The testing laboratory can **simulate** an actual aircraft landing.*

En route, On route

En route, meaning on the way, is the correct phrase.
*We were told the package is **en route** from the factory.*

Enclose, Inclose

Enclose is preferred in American usage.
*Please **enclose** your latest resume with the job application.*

Endemic, Epidemic

Endemic means peculiar to a given country or people.
*The fish are **endemic** to the waters of the Hawaiian Islands.*

An **epidemic** is something, usually a disease, that breaks out suddenly and affects many people.
*The polio **epidemic** still plagues some communities.*

Endless, Innumerable

Endless means without end, boundless, or interminable.
*The therapy prevents injury with an **endless** array of exercises.*

Innumerable means too many to count (countless).
*Yoga offers **innumerable** benefits to those seeking good health.*

Enervate, Innervate, Invigorate

Enervate means to drain energy or weaken something.
*The continuous hot and humid weather **enervated** all of us.*

Innervate means to stimulate a nerve or muscle.
*Atrophy occurs when the cells that **innervate** the muscle die.*

Invigorate means to energize something.
*The brisk morning swim **invigorated** Harry and Greg.*

Enormity, Enormousness

Enormity means immensely outrageous or wicked.
*The **enormity** of the defendant's crimes surprised the entire jury.*

Enormousness refers to an object's large size.
*The **enormousness** of the new county facility amazed us.*

Enough, Ample

See entry for **Ample, Enough**.

Enquire, Inquire

Inquire is the preferred spelling, but either is acceptable.

Ensure, Assure, Insure

See entry for **Assure, Ensure, Insure**.

Enthral, Enthrall

Enthrall, meaning to captivate, is preferred in American usage.
*Tom's second spy novel **enthralled** us more than his first novel.*

Enthused, Enthusiastic

Enthused is not popular with writing experts. Use **enthusiastic**.
*The students are **enthusiastic** (not **enthused**) about the new school.*

Entitled, Titled

Entitled means to have the right to something.
*Because she is the songwriter, she is **entitled** to the royalties.*

Titled refers to the name of a publication, speech, or musical piece.
*Their first musical piece this evening is **titled** "The Voice."*

Entomology, Etymology
Entomology is the study of insects. **Etymology** is the study of word origins.

Entrust, Intrust
Entrust is preferred in American usage.
*They **entrust** our firm with the management of their affairs.*

Enunciate, Annunciate
*See entry for **Annunciate, Enunciate**.*

Enure, Inure
Inure, meaning to get used to something undesirable, is preferred in American usage.
*We live in the woods, so we are **inured** to power outages.*

Envelop, Envelope
Envelop, a verb, means to enclose or surround.
*The mountain range was **enveloped** by raging fires last summer.*

Envelope, a noun, is the flat paper container for a letter.
*The special invitation arrived yesterday in a red **envelope**.*

Enviable, Envious
Enviable means worthy of envy.
*John Glenn has an **enviable** place in the history of space travel.*

Envious means showing envy.
*Some pilots are **envious** of John Glenn's mark on space travel.*

Epigram, Epigraph, Epitaph, Epithet
Epigram is a short humorous saying.
*Oscar Wilde wrote the **epigram**: "I can resist everything except temptation."*

Epigraph is a brief quotation at the beginning of a book or an inscription on a monument, statue, or building.
*The **epigraph** to E. M. Forster's novel* Howards End *is "Only connect!"*

Epitaph is a tribute to a dead person inscribed on a gravestone. *A famous* **epitaph** *on a poker player's gravestone reads, "He played five aces, now he plays the harp."*

Epithet is a short descriptive word or phrase applied to a person. *Bravery earned Richard Coeur de Lion the* **epithet** *"Lionheart."*

Equable, Equitable

Equable means unvarying, agreeable, or steady. *Ireland's* **equable** *climate is due to its proximity to the sea.*

Equitable means impartial, fair, or reasonable. *The club gave an* **equitable** *distribution of gifts to the charities.*

Equipment, Equipments

Use **equipment**. **Equipments** is not a word.

Equivocably, Equivocally

Equivocably is not a word.

Equivocate, Prevaricate, Procrastinate

Equivocate means to be deliberately ambiguous in order to mislead. *He* **equivocated** *and gave complex answers to our questions.*

Prevaricate means to stray from the truth, mislead, or lie. *He spoke with candor and saw no reason to* **prevaricate***.*

Procrastinate means to postpone, put off, or defer. *Why do the judges continue to* **procrastinate** *about a decision?*

Erasable, Irascible

Erasable means capable of being rubbed out or removed. *Please use only* **erasable** *markers on the white marker boards.*

Irascible means disagreeable or easily provoked. *After months of being unemployed, he became* **irascible***.*

Erode

Erode, Corrode
*See entry for **Corrode, Erode**.*

Errant, Arrant
*See entry for **Arrant, Errant**.*

Eruption, Irruption
Eruption refers to a violent outburst or discharge of material.
*The **eruption** of Mount Vesuvius destroyed Pompei in 79 AD.*

Irruption refers to an increase, such as in population.
*An **irruption** of winter finches from the north woods is expected.*

Escape goat, Scapegoat
Scapegoat, which is one who is blamed for another's misdeeds, is the correct word, though **escape goat** is actually closer to the original meaning of the phrase. It has roots in an ancient Jewish custom that allows one of two sacrificial goats to go free, taking the sins of the people with it. This goat was the *escaped goat*, which was later shortened to **scapegoat**.
*Making Jim the **scapegoat** for the team's loss is absurd.*

Especially, Specially
Especially means *particularly* or standing apart from all the rest.
*The air quality in the Adirondack Mountains is **especially** fresh.*

Specially means for a specific purpose or reason.
*Those students were **specially** chosen for their artistic talents.*

Essay, Assay
*See entry for **Assay, Essay**.*

Eternity, Affinity, Infinity
*See entry for **Affinity, Eternity, Infinity**.*

Euphemism, Euphuism

Euphemism is an inoffensive word or phrase substituted for an offensive word or phrase.
*The phrase "previously owned" is a **euphemism** for "used."*

Euphuism is a style of prose from the Elizabethan period.
*His writing style contrasts with the ornate style of **euphuism**.*

Eurhythmic, Arrhythmic

*See entry for **Arrhythmic, Eurhythmic**.*

Eventually, Ultimately

Eventually means at an unspecified time in the future.
*Holly knew that **eventually** she would make the honor roll.*

Ultimately means *at last* or the end result of something.
***Ultimately**, they had to give in to the manager's request.*

Ever so often, Every so often

Ever so often means frequently; **every so often** means occasionally.
*Be sure to check (**ever so often** or **every so often**) for news.*

Every day, Everyday

Every day means each day without an exception.
*We try to back up our hard drive **every day**.*

Everyday means ordinary, common, or not unusual.
*Problems are a natural **everyday** occurrence of life.*

Every one, Everyone

Every one means every person or thing without an exception.
*To their dismay, the deer ate **every one** of the shrubs.*

Everyone means all the people.
*Is **everyone** ready to begin the meeting?*

Evidence, Proof

Evidence is information that helps form a conclusion.
*Scientists have **evidence** that life could have existed on Mars.*

Proof is factual information that verifies a conclusion.
*His attorney uncovered **proof** of Joe's innocence.*

Evince, Evoke, Invoke

Evince means to exhibit or show something clearly.
*Paul McCartney **evinced** an amazing talent for music as a child.*

Evoke means to bring out something hidden or unexpressed.
*The music **evoked** many good memories of Molly's college days.*

Invoke means to call upon for help or to activate something.
*The defendant **invoked** the Fifth Amendment during the trial.*
*You can **invoke** that command by pressing the Enter key twice.*

Evocation, Avocation, Vocation

*See entry for **Avocation, Evocation, Vocation**.*

Ex-patriot, Expatriate

Expatriate is the correct word.

Exacerbate, Exasperate

Exacerbate means to make more violent, brutal, or severe.
*Closing the plant may **exacerbate** the bad mood in the town.*

Exasperate means to anger, irritate, or annoy.
*The voters were **exasperated** by the candidate's ignorance.*

Exalt, Exult

Exalt means to raise, praise, or elevate a person or thing.
*Let us **exalt** the brilliance of your achievements and ideas.*

Exult means to rejoice greatly.
*The professor **exulted** at being named department chairman.*

Exceed, Accede, Concede
See entry for **Accede, Concede, Exceed**.

Except, Accept
See entry for **Accept, Except**.

Exceptionable, Exceptional
Exceptionable means objectionable, offensive, or debatable.
We found their crude language quite **exceptionable**.
The court made some **exceptionable** *decisions today.*

Exceptional means uncommon, unusual, or extraordinary.
That student has an **exceptional** *memory for small details.*

Excess, Access
See entry for **Access, Excess**.

Exorbitant price, Exuberant price
Exorbitant price is the correct phrase.

Expand, Expend
Expand means to increase something.
The company's healthcare business **expanded** *by 50 percent.*

Expend means to lay out or spend.
The company **expended** *most of its effort on healthcare sales.*

Expatiate, Expiate
Expatiate means to write or speak at great length.
That company likes to **expatiate** *in detail about its products.*

Expiate means to atone or make amends for something.
He wanted to **expiate** *the guilt he felt all those years.*

Expect, Anticipate
See entry for **Anticipate, Expect**.

Expedient, Expeditious

Expedient means serving to promote or advance one's interest.
*It is **expedient** for him to start his re-election campaign early.*

Expeditious means acting with speed and efficiency.
*Please transfer the funds the most **expeditious** way.*

Explicit, Implicit

Explicit means clearly defined or stated.
*His surprising comments about the film are quite **explicit**.*

Implicit means implied or understood but not expressed.
*We have an **implicit** understanding with the building contractor.*

*Mel **expended** all of his money to **expand** his house.*

Expurgated, Abridged, Unabridged
See entry for **Abridged, Expurgated, Unabridged.**

Extant, Extent
Extant means still existing.
Few copies of Frank Sinatra's early albums are extant.

Extent means the measure of or limit of something.
We do not know the extent of the research done on the disease.

Extrapolate, Interpolate
Extrapolate means to estimate or predict from known information.
We can extrapolate from the data to determine an estimate.

Interpolate means to insert between.
The editor's suggestions are interpolated clearly in the margins.

F

All the fun's in how you say a thing. — Robert Frost

Fable, Legend, Myth

A **fable** is a simple, short, narrative story with animals as characters designed to enforce some useful truth or moral. A **legend** is an unverified story handed down from earlier times. A **myth** is a story usually dealing with a superhuman being and events that have no natural explanation.

Facetious, Factious, Factitious

Facetious means humorous or flippant.
*Cathy was being **facetious** with her stories and meant no harm.*

Factious means causing internal dissension or opposition.
*A **factious** attitude can hinder any workplace.*

Factitious means artificial or unnatural.
*Speculation caused the **factitious** value of those stocks.*
*The doctor ruled out malingering or a **factitious** disorder.*

Facilitate, Felicitate

Facilitate means to make easier.
*His assistant **facilitates** the ordering process.*

Felicitate means to congratulate or make happy.
*The league **felicitated** Jon on his 100th game.*

Faint, Feign, Feint

Faint, as an adjective, refers to being dizzy, lacking clarity, or lacking brightness. As a verb it means to lose consciousness.
*She suddenly felt **faint** after the rigorous workout in the gym.*
*He has a **faint** recollection of what happened last night.*
*The sun cast a **faint** shadow on the house at day's end.*
*Mom **fainted** when she learned about my award.*

Feign refers to giving a false appearance.
In the driving class, one student was asked to feign an injury.

Feint refers to a pretend punch in boxing.
Muhammad Ali used many feints against his opponents.

Fair to middling, Fair to midland

Fair to middling, meaning so-so, is the correct phrase. This late 1800s expression originally referred to cotton grading, where *fair* was one of the lowest grades of cotton and *middling* was the next lowest.

*Ben's mother **fainted** when she saw his **feigned** head injury.*

Famous, Infamous, Notorious

Famous means to be widely known.
*Tom Clancy, the **famous** author, autographed Eve's books.*

Infamous and **notorious** mean well known and unfavorably viewed.
*His philandering made him **infamous** (**notorious**) around town.*

Farther, Further

Farther refers to a physical distance.
*Do not place the unit **farther** than 10 feet from the house.*

Further refers to a greater degree or extent.
*Because of the legal aid ruling, the trial now faces **further** delay.*

Fatal, Fateful

Fatal refers to causing death, destruction, or ruin.
*By not heeding the advice, the group made a **fatal** mistake.*

Fateful refers to one's destiny.
*G. Lightfoot wrote about the Edmund Fitzgerald's **fateful** voyage.*

Father-in-laws, Fathers-in-law

Fathers-in-law is the correct phrase.

Faun, Fawn

Faun is a creature of Roman legend, part man and part goat.
*The **faun** is a disciple of the god Faunus.*

Fawn is a young deer usually less than a year old.
*If you see a **fawn** alone in a field, a doe is likely nearby.*

Faze, Phase

Faze means to disrupt or disturb something.
*The economic slowdown did not **faze** their business in any way.*

Phase, as a verb, means to carry out or conduct something. As a noun, **phase** is a stage of development.
*Mike is going to **phase** in the new procedures gradually.*
*The third **phase** of the building plan begins today.*

Fearful, Fearsome

Fearful means to be afraid of someone or something.
*They have grown more **fearful** about the year ahead.*

Fearsome means to cause fear in someone or something.
*A **fearsome** dog frightened the children.*

Fell swoop, Foul swoop

Fell swoop, which means all at once or suddenly, is the correct phrase. Coined by Shakespeare in his 1605 play *Macbeth*, the phrase originally referred to a bird's rapid descent upon prey.
*In one **fell swoop**, she provided all the data the client needed.*

Fervent, Fervid

Fervent means passionate or warm.
*It is our **fervent** wish that Bob quickly recovers from his illness.*

Fervid means impassioned or extremely hot.
*Peggy and Joe have a **fervid** dislike for extremely cold climates.*
*They endured the **fervid** temperatures of the tropical climate.*

Fever, Temperature

A person has a **fever** when his or her **temperature** is higher than 98.6° F.

Fewer, Less, Lest

Fewer refers to a number of individual persons or things.
Fewer than 50 applicants responded to the recent job vacancy.

Less refers to a quantity of something that cannot be counted as individual items.
*Because of drought, the fields are producing **less** corn this year.*

Note: If the number is only *one*, use **less**.
*One **less** person attended the meeting.*

Lest means *for fear that*.
Lest we forget, let's recognize Tom for his hard work right now.

Fiancé, Fiancée

Fiancé is a man engaged to be married. **Fiancée** is a woman engaged to be married.

Fictional, Fictitious

Fictional refers to fiction.
*Yoda is a **fictional** character in "The Empire Strikes Back."*

Fictitious refers to being imaginary or nonexistent.
*They're conducting business under assumed or **fictitious** names.*

Figuratively, Literally, Literately

Figuratively means metaphorically or symbolically.
***Figuratively** speaking, it is turning the business world on edge.*

Literally means following the exact meanings of the words.
*Several community volunteers **literally** built that house in two months.*

Literately is an adverb referring to the ability to read and write.
*We helped the **literately** impaired people learn the latest news.*

*Mom worried about the **fever** when baby's **temperature** topped 101°.*

Filipinos, Philippinos
People of the Philippines are referred to as **Filipinos**.

First, Firstly
First, an adverb, does not need an *ly*.
*First (not **firstly**), we could consider an alternative method.*
Note: This advice also applies to *secondly, thirdly, lastly,* etc.

First come – first serve, First come – first served
First come – first served is the correct phrase.

Flagrant, Blatant
*See entry for **Blatant, Flagrant**.*

Flair, Flare
Flair refers to a natural ability or aptitude to do something.
*She has a natural talent and **flair** for performing on stage.*

Flare refers to a bright light or flame.
*The police set up a road **flare** around the accident.*

Flambé, Flambeau
Flambé refers to food served with flaming liquor, and a **flambeau** is a large ornamental candlestick.

Flammable, Inflammable, Nonflammable
Flammable and **inflammable** are synonyms meaning burnable.
*Never light a match near a **flammable (inflammable)** liquid.*

Nonflammable means not flammable or not easily ignited.
*Trichlorofluoro methane is a colorless, **nonflammable** gas.*

Flatus, Afflatus
*See entry for **Afflatus, Flatus**.*

Flaunt

Flaunt, Flout

Flaunt means to display boastfully or to show off something.
*They **flaunt** their wealth by driving expensive cars to school.*

Flout means to ignore or show disrespect for rules.
*The haughty teens **flout** the most basic school rules.*

Flood, Deluge

See entry for ***Deluge, Flood***.

Florescent, Fluorescent

Florescent refers to a time of blossoming or flowering.
*His recent achievements indicate a **florescent** career in industry.*

Fluorescent means giving off light from radiation.
*Often **fluorescent** lights are used in greenhouses.*

Flotsam, Jetsam

Flotsam is floating cargo or wreckage following a shipwreck.
*The **flotsam** floated for weeks, long after the ship sank.*

Jetsam is something thrown overboard to lighten a ship in distress.
*The **jetsam** consisted of many cartons of canned food.*

Flounder, Founder

Flounder means to behave awkwardly or move in a clumsy way.
*The key witness **floundered** during her testimony.*

Founder means to sink or collapse.
*On its approach, the boat struck a reef and quickly **foundered**.*
*The prosecutor's case **foundered** after a key witness' testimony.*

Forbear, Forebear

Forbear, a verb, means to abstain or refrain from something.
*We **forbear** from making any negative comments about them.*

Forebear, a noun, means an ancestor.
*One of my **forebears** came to America on the Mayflower.*

Forbid, Prohibit

Both of these verbs mean refusing to allow something.

Forbid is usually used in cases of more personal situations.
*Their coach **forbids** them missing any of the Saturday practices.*

Prohibit is usually used in cases of lawful situations.
*The school **prohibits** them from leaving the grounds at lunch.*

Forbidding, Foreboding

Forbidding means unpleasant, often with the connotation that something is being prevented or slowed.
*He gave us a **forbidding** look when we asked about our bill.*
*The **forbidding** traffic made us late for the game.*

Foreboding is a premonition about something (usually negative).
*She had a **foreboding** her husband would be injured on the job.*

Forceful, Forcible

Forceful means powerful, vigorous, or effective.
*His **forceful** personality dominates much of the interview.*

Forcible means exercising by force or violence.
*The firefighters made a **forcible** entry into the burning building.*

Forego, Forgo

Forego means to go before in place or time.
*Her competent work and reputation always **forego** her.*
*It is a **foregone** conclusion that John will retire this year.*

Forgo means to give up, do without, or relinquish something.
*To compete in running races, you should **forgo** fatty foods.*

Foreword, Introduction, Preface

The **foreword** (not *forward*) of a book is a short note at the beginning of a book that usually tells how the book originated. Alternately, a **foreword** is a short introductory note written by someone other than the author. The **preface** is a statement written by the author about the book's objective or purpose. An

111

introduction, which can be written by the author or another person, follows the foreword and preface and tells the reader what to expect in the book.

Forgetful, Oblivious

Forgetful refers to a tendency not to remember.
*We found that **forgetful** behavior is common after the illness.*

Oblivious refers to being unaware or unmindful of something.
*They are **oblivious** to the fact that cameras are filming them.*

Formally, Formerly

Formally means in a traditional or formal manner.
*Celeste and Daniel are dressed **formally** for the occasion.*

Formerly means in the past.
*Jesse Ventura was **formerly** known as "The Body."*

Former, Latter

Former refers to the first of two and **latter** the second of two (or last of many). Note that when you use these words, the reader must remember what was written. This can sometimes be annoying, so you might want to reconsider using these words.

Formula, Formulae, Formulas

Formula is the singular form and **formulae** and **formulas** are the plural forms (**formulas** is more common).
*We're applying geometric **formulas** for finding the area.*

Fortuitous, Fortunate

Fortuitous means happening by chance or random, often with a positive connotation.
*The **fortuitous** software sales caused a rise in revenue.*

Fortunate means being lucky or having good fortune.
*She is **fortunate** that her unemployment lasted just a few months.*

Forward, Forwards

Forward means to be toward the front or to send on.
Please step forward when your name is called.
Please forward the bill to the customer's new home address.

Forwards is not preferred in American usage. Use **forward** instead.

Fragment, Fragmentary

Fragment refers to a small part detached from something.
That meteorite may be a fragment of a primitive asteroid.

Fragmentary refers to disconnected or incomplete parts.
It is possible to reconstruct organisms from fragmentary remains.

Frantically, Franticly

Frantically is preferred in American usage.

Free, Freely

Free means without charge.
Both the faculty and the students are admitted to the game free.

Freely, an adverb, means in a free manner or without any restrictions.
They freely voiced their opinions to their boss.

Freeze, Frieze

Freeze means to change a liquid into a solid, to stop, or to exclude.
Salt water freezes at a lower temperature than pure water.
When I access the Internet, my computer tends to freeze.
The higher park fees could freeze out the lower income families.

Frieze refers to an ornament.
A frieze that shows the history of the city is hung in the hallway.

Friend, Acquaintance

*See entry for **Acquaintance, Friend**.*

Frontward, Frontwards

Frontward is preferred in American usage.

Fulsome, Abundant

*See entry for **Abundant, Fulsome**.*

Funeral, Funerary, Funereal

Funeral refers to the service held for a dead person.
*The **funeral** was a celebration of his life.*

Funerary means associated with burial.
*The anthropologist studied the **funerary** beliefs of 500 years ago.*

Funereal means like a funeral, suggestive of death, gloomy, or sad.
*Where earlier the tone was quite **funereal**, now it feels uplifting.*

Fungous, Fungus

Fungous is the adjective (***fungous** diseases of plants*) and **fungus** is the noun (***fungus** can grow in damp environments*).

G

When ideas fail, words come in very handy.
                                    – Johann Wolfgang von Goethe

Gabardine, Gaberdine

Gabardine, a durable fabric with a twill weave, is preferred in American usage.
*Daniel is wearing his blue **gabardine** slacks to the interview.*

Gaff, Gaffe

Gaff is an iron hook attached to a pole usually used to grab large fish.
*The seaman uses a **gaff** to pull in the large tuna.*

Gaffe is a social error, blunder, or indiscreet remark (faux pas).
*I made a **gaffe** by mispronouncing my supervisor's last name.*

Gallop, Galop

Gallop refers to a fast gait or doing something quickly. **Galop** is an old word that refers to a lively dance.

Gamble, Gambol

Gamble means to risk, chance, or bet on something.
*I would not **gamble** my rent money at the casino.*

To **gambol** means to leap and skip about playfully.
*The children are joyfully **gamboling** around the school yard.*

Gantlet, Gauntlet

Gantlet, an old form of punishment, requires a person to run between two lines of people who flog him as he passes.
*Thieves were once made to run the **gantlet** as their punishment.*

Gauntlet refers to a heavy armored glove worn in medieval times. It is often used figuratively to mean a challenge, as in *he threw down the **gauntlet***.

Garnish, Garnishee

Garnish means to enhance in appearance or decorate something (most commonly food).
His broad-toed shoes were garnished with gold buckles.
The plate was garnished with a parsley sprig.

Garnishee, a legal term, means to seize someone's property or money.
The loan company garnisheed the deadbeat's wages.

Genial, Congenial, Congenital

See entry for Congenial, Congenital, Genial.

Genius, Genus

Genius is a person with exceptional ability, intelligence, or talent.
Surprisingly, Albert Einstein was not considered a boy genius.

Genus is a category, class, or type in taxonomy.
The museum lists all the plants by both genus and species.

Get my dander up, Get my dandruff up

Get my dander up is the correct expression. It means angry, and originates from the 1800s Dutch phrase *op donderon*, which means to burst into a sudden rage.
Those needless delays at the airport really get my dander up.

Gibe, Jibe

Gibe means to jeer, mock, or tease a person.
Eric sometimes gibes him about his unfortunate four-putt green.

Jibe means to agree with something.
Her independent audit jibes well with our accounting numbers.

Gild, Guild

Gild means to cover with a golden appearance.
The beautiful Canadian sunset gilded the grass in the valley.

Guild refers to an association of trades people.
Steven Spielberg is a member of the Directors Guild of America.

Gilt, Guilt

Gilt, as an adjective, means covered with gold (from the verb *gild*).
*She is wearing an elaborate **gilt** necklace to the party.*

Gilt, as a noun, refers to a thin gold covering or layer.
*Over the years much of the **gilt** wore away from the necklace.*

Guilt, a noun, is the responsibility for a wrongdoing or error.
*His **guilt** in the crime was proved by the prosecutor.*

Gist, Jest

Gist refers to the central idea of something.
*I understand the **gist** of what Tommy is trying to say.*

Jest refers to a joke.
*I spoke in **jest**, but Jane was offended by my comments.*

Gluten, Glutton

Gluten is a protein substance found in corn and wheat cereal grains.
*A strict **gluten**-free diet can improve a person's health.*

Glutton is someone who eats or drinks to excess, or someone who has a great capacity for enduring something.
*"I am not a **glutton**. I am an explorer of food."* – Erma Bombeck
*You must be a **glutton** for pain to run another marathon.*

Gone, Went

Gone must always be preceded by one of the 23 auxiliary (or helping) verbs (*are, was, were, have,* and others). **Went** never takes an auxiliary (or helping) verb.
*I should **have gone** to college when I had the chance.*
*I **went** to college immediately after high school.*

Note: The 23 auxiliary (or helping) verbs are: *am, are, be, being, been, can, could, did, do, does, had, has, have, is, may, might, must, shall, should, was, were, will,* and *would*.

Good, Well

Good is an adjective.
Debbie has always been a good elementary teacher.

Well can be an adjective (referring to one's health) or an adverb.
A few of the students do not look well today.
Debbie has always taught the students well.

Gored, Gourd

Gored refers to piercing, stabbing, or wounding with a pointed instrument (spear). **Gourd** refers to any of numerous hard-rinded inedible fruits.

Gorilla, Guerrilla

Gorilla refers to a large ape. **Guerrilla** refers to a member (soldier) of an independent armed resistance force.

*The **guerrilla** warily eyed the **gorilla**.*

Gourmand, Gourmet

Gourmand refers to someone who is fond of food and drink.
Brian is quite a gourmand and never skimps in his shopping.

Gourmet refers to a connoisseur of fine food and drink.
Being a gourmet is one requirement for a TV cooking expert.

Graduated, Graduated from

Graduated from is the correct phrase.
With high honors, I graduated from the University at Albany.

Grammar, Syntax

Grammar is the complete study of a language. **Syntax** is a part of grammar that deals with how words form phrases, clauses, and sentences.

Grateful, Gratified, Gratuitous

Grateful means to feel gratitude.
Many parents are grateful for the principal's intervention.

Gratified means to give pleasure or satisfy.
Walter's achievements in high school gratified his parents.

Gratuitous means free, unjustified, or unwanted.
His gratuitous advice on writing bored the veteran journalists.

Great Britain, British Isles, United Kingdom

See entry for **British Isles, Great Britain, United Kingdom.**

Grisly, Gristly, Grizzled, Grizzly

Grisly means ghastly or gruesome.
The prosecutor painted a grisly picture of the event.

Gristly means composed of or containing gristle.
The children gave the dog the gristly end to chew.

Grizzled means partly gray or streaked with gray.
Our leader today is a grizzled veteran of many mountain climbs.

Grizzly is a bear.
The grizzly bear is the greatest symbol of the wilderness.

Guarantee, Guaranty

Guarantee, a noun or verb, refers to assurance or security.
The store offers a one-year **guarantee** *on the used appliance.*
The manufacturer **guarantees** *the stove for one year.*

Guaranty, a noun, also means assurance or security.
The salesperson's record is a **guaranty** *of his honesty with clients.*

H

A word is not a crystal, transparent and unchanging. It is the skin of living thought.

— Oliver Wendell Holmes, Jr.

Habitant, Habitat, Inhabitant

Habitant and **inhabitant** both mean a person or animal who lives in a given area.
*Few **habitants** (**inhabitants**) of that area escaped the storm.*

Habitat is the environment of a person, animal, or plant.
*Johnny supports organizations that conserve **habitat** for wildlife.*

Hangar, Hanger

A **hangar** is a building that houses things like airplanes, and a **hanger** is a device used for hanging items like clothes.

Hanged, Hung

Hanged means executed by hanging.
*The five conspirators in the Lincoln assassination were **hanged**.*

Hung means suspended.
*The Christmas stockings are **hung** by the chimney with care.*

Note: Some word authorities accept **hung** as meaning executed.

Harbinger, Harbringer

Harbinger is the correct word.

Harbor, Port

A **harbor** is a body of water that protects ships. A **port** is a place where ships load and unload their cargo.

Harebrained, Hairbrained

The correct word is **harebrained**, meaning having no more sense than a *hare* (rabbit).

Hate, Despise

See entry for **Despise, Hate**.

Healthful, Healthy

Healthful means conducive to good health.
*Because of its **healthful** climate, we chose to live there all year.*

Healthy means possessing good health.
*Diet, exercise, and rest keep them **healthy** and energetic.*

Memory hook: Things are **healthful**; people and animals are **healthy**.

Hear, hear/Here, here

Hear, hear, an expression indicating approval, is the correct phrase.

Heart-rendering, Heart-rending

Heart-rending is the correct phrase.
*It's definitely one of the most **heart-rending** films we've seen.*

Height, Heighth

The correct spelling today is **height**, though years ago the word ended in *th*.

Hence, Thence, Whence

Hence means from here, from now, or thus.
*Two years **hence** this entire episode will be forgotten by all.*
*It is going to rain, **hence** the high humidity and clouds.*

Thence means from that time or from that place.
*We flew to Raleigh and **thence** to Dallas on our way back.*

Whence (an old word) means from what place, source, or cause.
***Whence** came all this valuable information?*

Herbivorous, Carnivorous, Omnivorous
See entry for **Carnivorous, Herbivorous, Omnivorous.**

Herein, Herewith
Both words are business jargon and should be avoided in writing. They have **enclosed** (not **herein** or **herewith**) receipts for all travel expenses.

Heritage, Hermitage
Heritage refers to inherited property, status acquired through birth, or a tradition. **Hermitage** refers to a place where one can live in seclusion (an abbey or monastery).

Heroin, Heroine
Heroin is a drug. **Heroine** is the principal female character in a novel, poem, or drama. It can also refer to a woman noted for courage, daring action, or special achievement.

Historic, Historical
Historic refers to something important or memorable.
The opening of the wing is a historic occasion for the hospital.

Historical means concerned with or relating to history.
Margaret Mitchell's "Gone with the Wind" is a historical novel.

Hoard, Horde
Hoard refers to a hidden find or cache.
Jim found a hoard of Roman coins with his metal detector.

Horde refers to a crowd or throng.
We ran into a horde of mosquitoes at last night's softball game.

Home, House
Home refers to intangible things (emotions) within a dwelling.
It's obvious they are all being raised in a very happy home.

House refers to a structure that can be built, bought, or sold.
The real estate broker just put their house on the market.

123

Home in on, Hone in on

Home in on, meaning to aim at a target, is the correct phrase.
*With that obvious clue, we can quickly **home in on** the answer.*

Homogeneous, Homogenous

Homogeneous means of the same or similar nature or kind.
*It was a **homogeneous** club, its members having similar values.*

Homogenous means resembling in structure, due to descent.
*As shown by their like physiology, the animals are **homogenous**.*

Homographs, Homophones

Homographs are words spelled alike but different in meaning
and pronunciation (noun *project* vs. the verb *project*).

Homophones are words pronounced alike but different in
spelling and meaning (*their, there* and *real, reel*).

*The **horde** of miners found a **hoard** of gold coins.*

Hostel, Hostile

Hostel refers to an inexpensive hotel usually for young travelers.
*Pete reserved his **hostel** online to ensure he had a place to stay.*

Hostile refers to being exceptionally unfriendly or antagonistic.
*The **hostile** forces failed to sabotage the revolution.*

How ever, However

How ever is used for emphasis.
***How ever** did you get front row seats for the concert?*

However means in whatever manner or *nevertheless*.
***However** the board decides, we probably should just accept it.*
***However**, the board should make a decision on the matter soon.*

Hue, Shade, Tint

Hue is a color's intensity. **Shade** is a degree of darkness of a color. **Tint** is a pale variation of a color.

Humerus, Humorous

Humerus is the long bone of the upper arm that extends from the shoulder to the elbow. **Humorous** means funny or amusing.

Hurdle, Hurtle

Hurdle refers to a difficulty or obstacle.
*The Health Care Bill cleared a big **hurdle** in the Senate today.*

Hurtle means to move with great speed or to go violently.
*Many baby boomers are **hurtling** toward their retirement age.*
*The tornado sent debris **hurtling** all over the community.*

Hurricane, Typhoon

A **hurricane** is a severe tropical storm that starts east of the International Date Line (Atlantic Ocean, Caribbean Sea, or Gulf of Mexico). A **typhoon** is a severe tropical storm that starts west of the International Date Line (Pacific Ocean or China Sea).

Hypercritical, Hypocritical

Hypercritical means overly critical, excessively exact, or picky. *His **hypercritical** movie review has the producers concerned.*

Hypocritical means two-faced or practicing hypocrisy. *It may be **hypocritical** of the newspaper to criticize the paparazzi.*

I

Half my life is an act of revision.   – John Irving

Ice tea, Iced tea
Iced tea is the correct phrase.

If I was, If I were
If I were is the correct phrase when one is referring to a conditional future event.
If I were president, I would stress feeding the hungry.

Ignorant, Stupid
Ignorant means not having learned.
*They tend to assume that people in earlier times were **ignorant**.*

Stupid means not able to learn.
*The worker was uneducated, but not necessarily **stupid**.*

Illegal, Illicit, Elicit
See entry for **Elicit, Illegal, Illicit**.

Illegible, Unreadable
Illegible means impossible to read because the words cannot be made out.
*For me, not the pharmacist, the prescription is **illegible**.*

Unreadable means the material is uninteresting or poorly written.
*The grammatical errors made the letter simply **unreadable**.*

Illiterate, Alliterate
See entry for **Alliterate, Illiterate**.

Illusion, Delusion, Allusion
See entry for **Allusion, Delusion, Illusion**.

Illusive, Elusive

*See entry for **Elusive, Illusive**.*

Imaginary, Imaginative

Imaginary means not real.
Imaginary friends are typical for kids between ages 3 and 6.

Imaginative means to show an imagination.
*Jim Henson's **imaginative** ability brought joy to many families.*

Immanent, Imminent, Eminent

*See entry for **Eminent, Immanent, Imminent**.*

Immature, Premature

Immature means not developed or fully grown.
*That child appears **immature** compared to the rest of the class.*

Premature means before the expected time (too soon).
*The **premature** infant was born at only seven months.*

Immemorial, Immortal

Immemorial means ancient beyond memory.
*His family had farmed that land since time **immemorial**.*

Immortal means deathless or eternal.
*In literature, Shakespeare is a true **immortal**.*

Immerge, Immerse, Emerge

*See entry for **Emerge, Immerge, Immerse**.*

Immigrant, Emigrant, Migrant

*See entry for **Emigrant, Immigrant, Migrant**.*

Immoral, Amoral

*See entry for **Amoral, Immoral**.*

Immunity, Impunity

Immunity means exempt from disease or obligation.
*The new vaccine provides **immunity** against chicken pox.*
*The church was granted **immunity** from any local taxation.*

Impunity means exempt from harm, penalty, or punishment.
*The favorite child teased his brother with **impunity**.*

Impartable, Impartible

Impartable means capable of being transmitted, communicated, or shared.
*The blacksmith's knowledge is **impartable**, if only we listen.*

Impartible means not divisible or not subject to partition.
*The children were sad to learn their father's estate is **impartible**.*

Impassable, Impassible

Impassable means not passable or unable to be traveled over.
*The road is **impassable** in winter and early spring.*

Impassible, a theological term, means incapable of suffering.
*He believes God does not suffer and is therefore **impassible**.*

Impel, Induce

Impel means to force an action.
*Factories are **impelled** to follow the environmental regulations.*

Induce means to persuade or to cause to do something.
*The doctor prescribed a mild drug to **induce** sleep.*

Imperial, Empirical

*See entry for **Empirical, Imperial**.*

Implicit, Explicit

*See entry for **Explicit, Implicit**.*

Imply, Infer

Imply means to convey or suggest a meaning indirectly.
*Her memo **implies** that the project would be delayed a week.*

Infer means to conclude from facts or premises.
*She **infers** from the evidence that the accused is not guilty.*

Memory hook: Speakers and writers **imply**; listeners and readers **infer**.

Impostor, Imposture

An **impostor** is a person who pretends to be someone else.
*The **impostor** felt he could bluff his way through the checkpoint.*

Imposture is the act of deception.
*Laws exist against the **imposture** of hyping worthless stocks.*

Impracticable, Impractical

Impracticable means not capable of being done.
*The extensive damage made repairing the car **impracticable**.*

Impractical means having little practical value.
*A plan for a new stadium would be seen as **impractical**.*

Impulsive, Compulsive, Compulsory

*See entry for **Compulsive, Compulsory, Impulsive**.*

In depth, Indepth

In depth must always be two words.
*Let us take an **in depth** look at news stories.*

In fact, Infact

In fact is always two words.
__In fact__, it's a surprise the team scores as well as it does.

In regard to, In regards to
In regard to, without an *s*, is the correct phrase. Sometimes you can avoid this phrase by substituting words like *on, about,* or *concerning.*
*He notified us **in regard to** (on, about, concerning) the change.*

In tact, Intact
Intact is always one word.

In the fact that, By the fact that
*See entry for **By the fact that, In the fact that**.*

In the same vane, In the same vein
In the same vein, which means similar or on the same topic, is the correct phrase.
*Author Jack Higgins writes **in the same vein** as Ian Fleming.*

Inalienable, Unalienable
Either word is correct, but **inalienable** is more common today.

Inanition, Inanity
Inanition is a lack of vitality or spirit, or exhaustion from hunger.
*The cheerleaders' **inanition** irritated the basketball coach.*
*The report details how the prisoners were starved into **inanition**.*

Inanity is a total lack of meaning, ideas, or sense.
*He resented the **inanity** of the tasks that were given to him daily.*

Inapt, Inept
Inapt means inappropriate or unsuitable.
*The only flaw in the film is an **inapt** and annoying soundtrack.*

Inept means awkward, clumsy, or uncoordinated.
*His **inept** words during the speech made him look incompetent.*

Incident, Accident, Mishap
*See entry for **Accident, Incident, Mishap**.*

Incidentally, Incidently
Incidentally means by chance or not intentionally. The word is commonly used to indicate that something is related, but not pertinent, to a topic being discussed.
*We like cheese. **Incidentally**, cheese has lots of calcium.*

Incidently is not a word.

Incipient, Insipid, Insipient
Incipient means emerging, developing, or initial.
*During the exam, the doctor recognized an **incipient** cancer.*

Insipid means dull, without flavor.
*The play's dialogue was **insipid**, so we left at intermission.*

Insipient means stupid or foolish.
*The article incisively pinpoints some of their **insipient** decisions.*

Incisive, Decided, Decisive
*See entry for **Decided, Decisive, Incisive**.*

Incite, Insight
Incite means to arouse or provoke action.
*Some political views tend to **incite** debate within a party.*

Insight refers to mental vision or understanding.
*Harold is offering his own **insights** on how to invest carefully.*

Inclose, Enclose
Enclose is preferred in American usage.
*Make sure you **enclose** your latest resume with the application.*

Inconceivable, Unthinkable
Inconceivable means incapable of being comprehended or explained.
*It's **inconceivable** that the merger will cost $30 billion.*

Unthinkable refers to something so undesirable or difficult to believe that it is unimaginable.
*It was once **unthinkable** for a man to go outside without a hat.*

Incredible, Incredulous

Incredible means hard to believe or unbelievable.
*Ed's quick explanation of the car accident is simply **incredible**.*

Incredulous means not believing or skeptical.
*Rob's story of flying saucers received a few **incredulous** stares.*

Indeterminable, Indeterminate

Indeterminable means impossible to fix, measure, or decide.
*The impact on the number of applications is **indeterminable**.*

Indeterminate means vague or unclear.
*Objects with **indeterminate** boundaries are difficult to model.*

Indict, Indite

Indict means to accuse or formally charge.
*The grand jury is going to **indict** the suspect this week.*

Indite means to compose or put into writing.
*Our boss seldom uses a writer to help **indite** his speeches.*

Indictment, Arraignment

*See entry for **Arraignment, Indictment**.*

Indifferent, Ambiguous, Ambivalent

*See entry for **Ambiguous, Ambivalent, Indifferent**.*

Indigenous, Indigent, Indignant

Indigenous means native.
***Indigenous** cultures can often contribute to medical discoveries.*

Indigent means in need of money, impoverished, or poor.
*The government provides medical care for **indigent** families.*

Indignant means angry.
*A full and detailed explanation backs Phil's **indignant** denial.*

Indiscreet, Indiscrete

Indiscreet means not showing prudent or good judgment.
*His open discussion of their financial problems was **indiscreet**.*

Indiscrete means not divided or divisible into separate parts.
*The soil consisted of **indiscrete** layers of sand, dirt, and gravel.*

Inductive, Deductive

*See entry for **Deductive, Inductive**.*

Inequity, Iniquity

Inequity refers to injustice or unfairness.
*Many voters are unhappy about the **inequity** of the system.*

Iniquity refers to immorality, sin, or wickedness.
*The tribunal sought to investigate the dictator's many **iniquities**.*

Inexpensive, Cheap

*See entry for **Cheap, Inexpensive**.*

Inexplicable, Inextricable

Inexplicable means difficult or impossible to explain.
*The TV show's **inexplicable** popularity pleases the sponsors.*

Inextricable means difficult or impossible to separate or avoid.
*The conflict is **inextricably** linked to poor communication.*

Infamous, Famous, Notorious

*See entry for **Famous, Infamous, Notorious**.*

Infectious, Contagious

*See entry for **Contagious, Infectious**.*

Infinity, Affinity, Eternity

*See entry for **Affinity, Eternity, Infinity**.*

Inflammable, Flammable, Nonflammable

*See entry for **Flammable, Inflammable, Nonflammable**.*

Inflict, Afflict
*See entry for **Afflict, Inflict**.*

Inform, Advise
*See entry for **Advise, Inform**.*

Informant, Informer
Informant is a person who gives information.
*We just learned that the **informant** was our neighbor.*

Informer is a person who is paid for information about others.
*The **informer** testified against Frank.*

Ingenious, Ingenuous, Disingenuous
*See entry for **Disingenuous, Ingenious, Ingenuous**.*

Inhabitant, Habitant, Habitat
*See entry for **Habitant, Habitat, Inhabitant**.*

Inhuman, Inhumane
Inhuman means lacking human qualities such as kindness or pity.
*It was **inhuman** of them to deprive him of time with his family.*

Inhumane means being cruel or insensitive to others.
*Many read about the **inhumane** treatment of the prisoners.*

Inimical, Inimitable
Inimical means harmful, hostile, or unfriendly.
*Their polices were **inimical** to democratic principles.*

Inimitable means defying imitation or matchless.
*The comedian entertained the audience in his **inimitable** way.*

Innervate, Enervate, Invigorate
*See entry for **Enervate, Innervate, Invigorate**.*

Innumerable

Innumerable, Endless
See entry for Endless, Innumerable.

Inquire, Enquire
Inquire is the preferred spelling, but either is acceptable.

Insidious, Invidious
Insidious means spreading harm in a subtle way.
Her criticism has an insidious effect on the team's morale.

Invidious means being discriminatory or causing resentment.
The new laws appear to be unjust and invidious to many people.

Insoluble, Insolvable, Insolvent
Insoluble means it cannot be dissolved.
The high-protein soy powder is insoluble in milk.

Insolvable means not easily solved.
The corporation continues to have insolvable quality problems.

Insolvent means incapable of paying debts.
The owners are selling the assets of those insolvent companies.

Install, Instill
Install means to put into position or to set up.
Katie is going to install the new software after work.

Instill means to implant or introduce gradually.
The short preparation is not enough time to instill confidence.

Instinct, Intuition
Instinct is an inborn tendency within an individual.
A bear's instinct makes the animal hibernate in the winter.

Intuition is knowledge of something without the use of reason.
Brett's intuition told him to sell the stock before it crashed.

Insure, Assure, Ensure
See entry for Assure, Ensure, Insure.

Intense, Intensive

Intense means occurring in an extreme degree or powerful.
*The heat last summer was so **intense**, several people died.*

Intensive means concentrated or thorough.
*The **intensive** care he got helped him recover from the accident.*

Intentionally, Advisedly

*See entry for **Advisedly, Intentionally**.*

Interment, Internment

Interment refers to a burial.
*The **interment** takes place soon after the religious service.*

Internment refers to confinement or imprisonment, without trial, of an enemy.
*The agency complained about the **internment** of the civilian.*

Intermittent, Occasional

Intermittent means starting and stopping at intervals.
***Intermittent** acute sun exposure can damage the skin.*

Occasional means infrequent or irregular.
*The **occasional** wash and wax won't keep my car looking good.*

Internet, Intranet

Internet, always capitalized, is a worldwide system of computer networks. **Intranet**, which doesn't need to be capitalized, is a much smaller and private network within an enterprise. Note that the rarer term, *extranet*, can be viewed as a subset to a company's **intranet** that is extended to users outside the company.

Interpolate, Extrapolate

*See entry for **Extrapolate, Interpolate**.*

Interpret, Interpretate

Interpretate is not a word.

Interpreter, Translator
An **interpreter** converts speech to another language, and a **translator** converts writing to another language.

Interstate, Intestate, Intrastate
Interstate means between states.
The interstate long distance rate drops on the weekends.

Intestate means without a will.
The law of intestate succession can vary from state to state.

Intrastate means within one state.
The bill attempts to specifically regulate intrastate commerce.

Intolerable, Intolerant
Intolerable means tiring or unbearable.
He considered the store's poor service intolerable.

Intolerant means biased, prejudiced, or unwilling to accept.
She was intolerant of people who didn't see things her way.

Introduction, Foreword, Preface
See entry for Foreword, Introduction, Preface.

Intrust, Entrust
See entry for Entrust, Intrust.

Inure, Enure
See entry for Enure, Inure.

Invent, Discover
See entry for Discover, Invent.

Invigorate, Enervate, Innervate
See entry for Enervate, Innervate, Invigorate.

Invoke, Evince, Evoke
See entry for Evince, Evoke, Invoke.

Inward, Inwards
Inward is preferred in American usage.

Irascible, Erasable
See entry for **Erasable, Irascible.**

Irregardless, Regardless
Irregardless is a nonstandard word. Avoid its use.

Regardless means without regard or unmindful.
The foursome plays every Saturday **regardless** *of the weather.*

Irrelevant, Irreverent
Irrelevant means not pertinent or not relating to the subject.
Some of the testimony in the case seemed to be **irrelevant.**

Irreverent means disrespectful, satirical, or lacking reverence.
The rowdy Cub Scouts' **irreverent** *behavior angered the scoutmaster.*

Irritate, Aggravate
See entry for **Aggravate, Irritate.**

Irruption, Eruption
See entry for **Eruption, Irruption.**

Isle, Aisle
See entry for **Aisle, Isle.**

Its, It's
Its is a possessive pronoun that is never split by an apostrophe.
Though outdated, our first computer has served **its** *purpose.*

It's is the contracted or shortened form of *it is.*
It's *definitely much faster than our first computer.*

Memory hook: Possessive **its** never *splits.*

Ivory tower, Ivy tower

Ivory tower, which refers to a remote place or an attitude of retreat, is the correct phrase. Originally inspired by the Bible's Song of Solomon, it was Henry James' 1916 novel of that title that embedded the phrase in the English vocabulary.

*What does he know about our situation, living as he does in an **ivory tower**?*

J

The most valuable of all talents is that of never using two words when one will do.

– Thomas Jefferson

Jail, Prison
A **jail** is a short-term detaining facility for those awaiting trial or for those convicted of minor offenses. A **prison**, sometimes referred to as a *penitentiary*, is a long-term detaining facility for those convicted of major offenses.

Jerry-built, Jury-built, Jerry-rigged, Jury-rigged
Jerry-built, which carries a negative connotation, refers to a permanent, but poorly built, construction. The origin of the phrase is unclear, but it may have derived from the flimsy work of an English construction company called Jerry Brothers. **Jury-rigged**, which dates to the late 1700s nautical term *jury mast*, refers to a ship's temporary mast. It means something cleverly constructed in a makeshift manner for temporary use. Sometimes these two expressions are misstated as **jerry-rigged** or **jury-built**.

Jest, Gist
See entry for **Gist, Jest**.

Jetsam, Flotsam
See entry for **Flotsam, Jetsam**.

Jibe, Gibe
See entry for **Gibe, Jibe**.

Judgement, Judgment
Judgment without the first e is preferred in American usage. *We reserve **judgment** until all the facts are available.*

Judicial, Judicious, Juridical

Judicial refers to the law courts or judges.
*The **judicial** branch is just one branch of the U.S. government.*

Judicious refers to a person's careful or wise judgment.
*The taxpayers want to see **judicious** spending.*

Juridical refers to the administration of justice.
*He proceeded to fulfill the **juridical** requirements of the case.*

Jump start, Kick start

Jump start refers to getting something started or revived, such as a weak economy. **Kick start** refers to starting a motorcycle.

K

Words are, of course, the most powerful drug used by mankind.

– Rudyard Kipling

Karat, Carat, Caret, Carrot
See entry for **Carat, Caret, Carrot, Karat.**

Kick start, Jump start
See entry for **Jump start, Kick start.**

Kind of, Sort of
Avoid these awkward phrases if you mean *somewhat.*
*The concert was somewhat (not **kind of** or **sort of**) boring.*

Kin, Kith
Kin refers to family or relatives. **Kith** refers to acquaintances, friends, or neighbors.

Know-how
Avoid this colloquial and informal phrase in formal writing.
*They have a reputation for exceptional knowledge (not **know-how**) on this topic.*

Koala bear
A **koala** is a marsupial, not a bear. Just call these animals **koalas**.

L

So difficult is it to show the various meanings and imperfections of words when we have nothing else but words to do it with.

– John Locke

Landslide, Avalanche
See entry for **Avalanche, Landslide**.

Languid, Limp, Limpid
Languid means lacking energy or vitality.
*With **languid** waves of the hand, they said their goodbyes.*

Limp, as an adjective, means lacking in stiffness.
*The **limp** lettuce ruined the chef's salad.*

Limpid means crystal clear.
__Limpid__ streams are found in this mountainous area.

Lapse, Elapse
See entry for **Elapse, Lapse**.

Latin Abbreviations
Here are some common Latin abbreviations and their meanings:

e.g. (exempli gratia) means *for example.*
etc. (et cetera) means *and other things.*
ibid (ibidem) means *in the same place.*
i.e. (id est) means *that is* or *that is to say.*

Latter, Former
See entry for **Former, Latter**.

Lawful, Legal

Lawful means rightful or in accordance with the law.
*The elder son is the **lawful** heir to much of the estate.*
*He transferred the ownership of the property in a **lawful** way.*

Legal means relating to the law.
*The **legal** arena is addressing the downloading of Internet music.*

Lay, Lie

Lay means to place or to put something; it requires a direct object.
*Where are you going to **lay** that book?*
*I am **laying** the book on the kitchen counter.*
*He **laid** the book on the kitchen counter.*

Lie means to be in a horizontal position; it never takes an object.
*The baseball **lies** in the street next to the car.*
*The baseball is **lying** by the car.*
*How long has the baseball **lain** in the street?*

*The chicken **lays** an egg while the farmer **lies** in the hay.*

Leaflet

Leaflet, Brochure, Pamphlet

See entry for Brochure, Leaflet, Pamphlet.

Leak, Leek

Leak refers to the escape or passage of something.
All of the water leaked out of his canteen while he was hiking.

Leek refers to an edible plant (part of the onion family).
Rick grew beets, tomatoes, and leeks in his garden.

Lean, Lien

Lean, as an adjective, means having a low fat content. As a verb, it means to incline.
Venison is lean compared with many meats we have eaten.
Do not lean against the door of the train.

Lien means a legal claim to something.
The bank has a lien against their vacation home in New Jersey.

Learn, Teach

Learn means to acquire information or knowledge.
This computer game helps people learn how to read.

Teach means to impart knowledge or information.
Some English teachers still teach how to diagram sentences.

Leastways, At least

See entry for At least, Leastways.

Leave, Let

Leave means to allow to remain or to go away.
If you leave the book with me, I'll be sure to read it.
If you leave quietly, no one in the library will be disturbed.

Let means to allow or to permit.
Please let me help you with your chemistry homework.

Note: When **leave** or **let** is used with the word *alone*, these words are interchangeable.
Leave (let) Gerry alone while he is doing his homework.

146

Lectern, Podium, Rostrum

Lectern is a small slanted stand that supports papers or books.
Podium is an elevated small platform where one stands.
Rostrum is also a platform but larger than a **podium** and usually more decorative.

Memory hook: You stand *behind* a **lectern** and *on* a **podium** or **rostrum**.

Legation, Ligation

Legation refers to the premises occupied by a diplomatic minister and staff.
*The French **legation** is the residence of the chargé d'affaires.*

Ligation refers to binding or applying a ligature (as in surgery).
***Ligation** and stripping is a surgery used on varicose veins.*

Legend, Fable, Myth

*See entry for **Fable, Legend, Myth.***

Legislator, Legislature

Legislator refers to a lawmaker.
*The **legislator** proposed a law that limits tobacco sales.*

Legislature refers to a group of lawmakers.
*The election brought 10 new members to the city **legislature**.*

Lend, Loan

Lend is a verb.
*Please **lend** me $20.*

Loan is a noun.
*The $20 is a gift, not a **loan**.*

Note: Although careful writers maintain this distinction, it is common to see **lend** and **loan** used interchangeably as verbs.

Less, Fewer, Lest

*See entry for **Fewer, Less, Lest.***

Lessee, Lessor

Lessee refers to a lease holder or tenant.
*The **lessee** makes the payments on the 15ᵗʰ of every month.*

Lessor refers to a lease grantor or landlord.
*The **lessor** keeps full ownership rights of the apartment.*

Lessen, Lesson

Lessen means to diminish or become less.
*My broker says bond funds may **lessen** investment risk.*

Lesson is something to be learned.
*The new software helps teachers make detailed **lesson** plans.*

Levee, Levy

Levee is a formal reception or an embankment.
*The new consul was introduced at a **levee** near the embassy.*
*After the **levee** broke, the town quickly evacuated.*

Levy, a verb, means to impose, enlist, or begin war.
*The court could **levy** a fine for misappropriating the funds.*
*They are going to **levy** troops from the countryside.*
*They want to avoid **levying** war at all costs.*

Levy, a noun, is a charge imposed or the act of levying money, property, or troops.
*The tax **levy** is a real challenge this year.*
*The recent **levy** enlisted few troops for the military.*

Liable, Libel, Lible, Slander

Liable means legally responsible or likely.
*The jury quickly found him **liable** for fraud.*
*Considering the dark clouds, it is **liable** to rain today.*

Libel is damaging someone's reputation in print or other media.
*The inaccurate story prompted him to sue for **libel**.*

Lible is not a word.

Slander is an oral statement that damages a person's reputation.
*His negative comments toward him were taken as **slander**.*

Ligament, Tendon

A **ligament** is the strong connective tissue that connects bones or cartilage at a joint. A **tendon** is the fibrous tissue that connects the muscle to the bone.

Lightening, Lightning

Lightening means making lighter.
*John can never be accused of **lightening** the workload.*

Lightning is an atmospheric electrical discharge.
*If you are not careful, golf clubs can act like **lightning** rods.*

Like, As

*See entry for **As, Like**.*

Likely, Apt

*See entry for **Apt, Likely**.*

Limit, Limitation

Limit refers to a physical or political boundary.
*They say there may be no **limit** to how long people can live.*

Limitation refers to a restraint or restriction.
*Some states have a **limitation** on cell phone use in cars.*

Linage, Lineage

Linage refers to the number of lines of printed material.
*The newspaper charges its advertisers by ad size and **linage**.*

Lineage refers to ancestry, line of descent, or derivation.
*The family could trace their **lineage** to the 14th century.*

Liqueur, Liquor

A **liqueur** (or cordial) is a sweet, strong, highly flavored alcoholic drink. A **liquor** is an alcoholic beverage (such as whiskey) made by distillation rather than by fermentation (such as wine or beer). **Liquor** is also a broth derived by cooking meats or vegetables for a long time.

Litany, Liturgy

Litany refers to a form of prayer or a lengthy list.
The Litany of the Saints is read at our church every Sunday.
The accused faced a litany of questions about his whereabouts.

Liturgy refers to the prescribed form for a religious service.
Today's worship service is built around the liturgy of celebration.

Literally, Figuratively, Literately

See entry for Figuratively, Literally, Literately.

Lo and behold, Low and behold

Lo and behold is the correct phrase.

Loath, Loathe

Loath means reluctant or unwilling.
Henry is loath to move despite the attractive job offer.

Loathe means to dislike intensely.
Every month we loathe receiving those credit card bills.

Locale, Locality, Location

Locale is a place associated with a particular event or occurrence.
The film producers found a locale in Mexico for the sequel.

Locality is a particular neighborhood, place, or district.
Our vacation house is in a quiet locality not far from the shore.

Location is a place where something is situated.
The location of the damaged part has not been determined.

Loose, Lose

Loose means unrestrained or not tight.
Giant icebergs continue to shake loose off the Antarctic coast.

Lose means to mislay or miss out on something.
By not accepting credit cards, companies can lose potential sales.

Loosen, Unloosen
Loosen is the correct word. The *un* is not needed.

Luxuriant, Luxurious
Luxuriant refers to something abundant, profuse, or rich.
Luxuriant lawns and gardens surround the hotel on all sides.

Luxurious refers to luxury.
*The vacation package includes a weekend stay at a **luxurious** hotel.*

M

I love writing. I love the swirl and swing of words as they tangle with human emotions.

– James A. Michener

Magnate, Magnet

Magnate is a powerful person (usually in business).
The shipping magnate donates money to cancer research.

Magnet is a person or thing that exerts attraction.
The low cost of living there is a magnet for the retired.

Magnificent, Magniloquent, Munificent

Magnificent means grand or splendid.
The Hearst Castle has a magnificent view of the ocean.

The shipping magnate plays with his favorite magnet.

Magniloquent means colorful, extravagant, or lofty in speech.
My professor's magniloquent talks are entertaining but confusing.

Munificent means extremely generous.
The celebrities gave a munificent donation to the relief effort.

Majority, Plurality

Majority means more than 50 percent.
The majority of the country favored last year's tax cut.

Plurality means the most of something, even if it is less than 50 percent.
Clinton won the Presidency with a plurality of the votes.

Maniac, Manic

Maniac is a crazy person, and **manic** is a clinical term referring to mania, excitement, or a psychological affliction (*manic depression*).

Mantel, Mantle

A **mantel** is a shelf (mantelpiece).
The couple placed a prized piece of art over their mantel.

A **mantle** is a cloak or something that covers like a cloak.
This morning a mantle of fog hung over the valley for a few hours.

Many, Much

Many refers to countable items or units.
Many students volunteered their time for the charity.

Much refers to noncountable items or units.
Low-octane fuel caused much of our car trouble.

Marked, Remarkable

Marked means clearly defined and evident.
We noticed that Jack has a marked limp when he walks.

Remarkable means extraordinary or worthy of notice.
We noticed a remarkable improvement in Gerry's grades.

Masseur, Masseuse
Masseur is a male massage therapist, and **masseuse** is a female massage therapist.

Masterful, Masterly
Masterful means domineering or powerful.
General George Patton was a masterful soldier and leader.

Masterly means highly skilled.
Her spring concert was a masterly performance of Bach.

Material, Materiel
Material is the substance from which something is composed.
His new suit is made of a light blue silk material.

Materiel is the equipment or supplies used by an organization.
The convoy brought materiel to the forward base.

May, Can, Could, Might
See entry for Can, Could, May, Might.

May be, Maybe
May be is a verb phrase indicating possibility.
On this matter, it may be necessary to ask for a second opinion.

Maybe is an adverb meaning *perhaps*.
Maybe the legal staff can resolve this issue within a few days.

May have, May of
May have is the correct phrase.
As you may have heard by now, tonight's class was cancelled.

Mayoral, Mayoralty
Mayoral (an adjective) refers to matters concerning the officer (mayor) or the office.
The mayoral election is in June, and it's already contentious.

Mayoralty (a noun) refers to the office or term of a mayor.
Mr. Daily was well suited for the mayoralty.

Mean, Median

Mean is the sum of all the numbers in a group divided by the number of figures. It is commonly called the *average*.
*The arithmetic **mean** of 1, 5, and 6 is (1+5+6) ÷ 3 = 4*

Median is the midpoint of a range of numbers. To find a median, write the numbers in order from largest to smallest. The figure with the same number of figures above and below is the median.
*The **median** of 12, 19, 23, 45, and 60 is 23.*

Mean, Mien

Mean, an adjective, means lacking kindness.
*Though the dog looks **mean**, he is just a playful puppy.*

Mien, a noun, refers to a person's manner or appearance.
*Annie is known for her noble **mien**, virtue, and great appeal.*

Meantime, Meanwhile

Both words refer to an intervening time.

Meantime is commonly used as a noun.
*In the **meantime**, we continue to wait for another opportunity.*

Meanwhile is commonly used as an adverb.
***Meanwhile**, we waited an extra hour for the children to arrive.*

Meddle, Mettle

Meddle means to interfere with something.
*We have no desire to **meddle** in the politics of our community.*

Mettle refers to the quality or strength of a person's character.
*Rachel is being given a chance to prove her **mettle** and worth.*

Media are, Media is

Media are is correct because *media* is the plural of *medium*.
*All the news **media are** covering the events of the trial.*

Mediate, Arbitrate, Adjudicate

*See entry for **Adjudicate, Arbitrate, Mediate**.*

Memento

Memento, Momento

Memento is a special remembrance or souvenir.
Joe brought back a memento from England for his wife.

Note: In Catholicism, **memento** refers to the Canon of the Mass.

Momento is not a word.

Mendacity, Mendicity

Mendacity refers to lying or dishonesty.
An odor of mendacity hung over his testimony at the hearing.

Mendicity means begging.
This law curbs behavior such as mendicity.

Meretricious, Meritorious

Meretricious means fake, flashy, or attractive in a bad way.
Though sharp, his arguments were deemed meretricious.

Meritorious means deserving of praise, reward, and honor.
The mayor recognized Jan for meritorious service to the town.

Meteorology, Metrology

Meteorology is the science of weather. **Metrology** is the science of measurement.

Method, Methodology

Method is a way to do something.
What method did the golf pro use to fix Bill's slice?

Methodology is a set of methods, procedures, or rules.
He introduced a different methodology of linguistics.

Meticulous, Scrupulous

Meticulous means exact, finicky, or precise.
The Binghamton artist shows a meticulous attention to detail.

Scrupulous means conscientious or principled.
A scrupulous character tries to stay within the letter of the law.

Might have, Might of
Might have is the correct phrase.
*Do you think they **might have** gone without him?*

Migrant, Emigrant, Immigrant
*See entry for **Emigrant, Immigrant, Migrant**.*

Militate, Mitigate
Militate means to influence or oppose something.
*The leader's anger **militated** against any hope of a truce.*

Mitigate means to diminish in severity or to lessen.
*The physical therapy for my neck **mitigated** the severe pain.*

Milk toast, Milquetoast
Milk toast refers to buttered toast usually served in warm milk with sugar and seasonings. **Milquetoast** refers to a shy, timid, or unassertive person. The origin of the word is a cartoon character, Caspar Milquetoast, who starred in Harold Webster's comic strip *The Timid Soul* (1924 to 1953).

Millenary, Millinery
Millenary refers to a thousand. **Millinery** refers to women's hats.

Minimize, Diminish
*See entry for **Diminish, Minimize**.*

Minion, Minyan
Minion is a subordinate, servant, follower, or dependent.
Minyan is a quorum, the number of adult Jewish men required for a communal religious service.

Miniscule, Minuscule
Minuscule is the preferred spelling.
*The thorough study shows the disadvantages are **minuscule**.*

Mishap

Mishap, Accident, Incident
See entry for **Accident, Incident, Mishap**.

Misinformation, Disinformation
See entry for **Disinformation, Misinformation**.

Misplace, Displace
See entry for **Displace, Misplace**.

Misuse, Abuse
See entry for **Abuse, Misuse**.

Mobile, Movable
Mobile means it can move and **movable** means it can *be* moved.

Moot point, Mute point
Moot point, a legal term dating to the mid 16th century, is the correct phrase. Then it specifically referred to hypothetical cases debated by law students. Because these debates were hypothetical, the phrase's meaning eventually changed to *not worth debating* or *of little significance*.

Moral, Morale
Moral, as an adjective, means righteous. As a noun, a **moral** is a principle.
*They continually show a **moral** dimension to their actions.*
*What **moral** or message can be drawn from today's reading?*

Morale refers to the spirit or state of mind.
*Despite the surprise loss, we maintain a high team **morale**.*

More important, More importantly
Prefer **more important** because the *ly* is unnecessary.
More important, we make education a fun experience.

The same guideline applies to the phrase *most importantly*.

More so, Moreso

Despite the frequent use of **moreso**, it is not a word. Always spell it as two words (**more so**).

More than, Over

More than refers to countable items.
More than 500 churches are in upstate New York.

Over refers to general amounts or unspecified increments.
Over half of the inventory was unsold, resulting in a huge loss.

Most, Almost

See entry for *Almost, Most*.

Mother-in-laws, Mothers-in-law

Mothers-in-law is the correct phrase.

Motto, Slogan

A **motto** is a short phrase that usually expresses a moral aim or purpose. A **slogan** is a catch phrase used by a political party, fraternity, or other organization in advertising or promotion.

Much, Muchly

Muchly is not a word.
*We would **much** (not **muchly**) appreciate your attendance.*

Mucus, Mucous

Mucus is the noun and **mucous** is the adjective.
Mucus is emanating from the mucous glands.

Multilateral, Bilateral, Unilateral

See entry for *Bilateral, Multilateral, Unilateral*.

Must have, Must of

Must have is the correct phrase.
*The bank **must have** seen that foreclosure coming for weeks.*

Mutant, Mutation

A **mutant** refers to an organism arising from a **mutation**. A **mutation** is a new physical characteristic arising from a genetic anomaly.

Mutual, Common, Ordinary, Popular

See entry for **Common, Mutual, Ordinary, Popular.**

Mysterious, Mystical

Mysterious means beyond human comprehension or unintelligible.
A **mysterious** craft appeared in the sky and left us wondering.

Mystical means hidden from human knowledge (spiritual).
The Blessed Mother's apparition at Fatima was a **mystical** experience.

Myth, Fable, Legend

See entry for **Fable, Legend, Myth.**

N

Those for whom words have lost their value are likely to find that ideas have also lost their value.

— Edwin Newman

Nation, Country
See entry for **Country, Nation**.

Naturalist, Naturist
A **naturalist** is someone interested in natural history, especially botany or zoology. A **naturist** is a person who practices nudity for reasons of health or religion.

Nauseated, Nauseous
Nauseated means to feel sick.
*Joe feels **nauseated** 20 minutes after his workout.*

Nauseous is an adjective meaning sickening.
*The neighbors refuse to put up with that **nauseous** stench.*

Neither, Either
See entry for **Either, Neither**.

Nibble, Nybble
Nibble refers to a quick, small bite or morsel of food. **Nybble** refers to four bits in computer terminology.

Nip it in the bud, Nip it in the butt
Nip it in the bud, meaning to stop something while it is still in development, is the correct expression. This phrase refers to the de-budding of plants, allowing the remaining buds to grow better.
*The boss wants to **nip** that questionable practice **in the bud**.*

No one
Always spell this as two words.
***No one** picks up the mail while we are away.*

No sooner than, No sooner when

No sooner than is correct. In this phrase, the word **sooner** is a comparative adverb and should be followed by **than** (not **when**).
*We had **no sooner** left the game **than** a batter hit a home run.*

Nohow

Nohow, nonstandard for *in no way* or *not at all*, should be avoided.
The clerk could in no way (not **nohow**) *decipher his handwriting.*

Noisome, Noisy

Noisome means foul-smelling, noxious, or offensive.
*The **noisome** odor coming from the river bothers the residents.*

Noisy means making much noise.
*Despite the PC's high price, the keyboard is quite **noisy**.*

Nonflammable, Flammable, Inflammable

*See entry for **Flammable, Inflammable, Nonflammable**.*

Northward, Northwards

Northward is preferred in American usage.

Notable, Noticeable

Notable means worthy of notice.
*Her accomplishments in chemistry are **notable**.*

Noticeable means readily observed.
*The construction crew is making **noticeable** progress.*

Notorious, Famous, Infamous

*See entry for **Famous, Infamous, Notorious**.*

Novice, Amateur

*See entry for **Amateur, Novice**.*

Nowhere near

Nowhere near is colloquial and should be avoided in writing.
Use not nearly or *does not approach* instead.

Nowhere, Nowheres
Always use **nowhere**.

Number, Amount
See entry for **Amount, Number.**

Numerable, Numerous
Numerable refers to something that can be counted or numbered.
If the data are not **numerable,** *the impact cannot be measured.*

Numerous means *a great number of* or *many.*
The election officials tried saving **numerous** *flawed ballots.*

The **noisome** *odor drifted into the* **noisy** *party.*

O

Language ought to be the joint creation of poets and manual workers.
– George Orwell

Oblivious, Obvious

Oblivious means unaware or unmindful of something.
*He was **oblivious** to the danger of the sun's ultraviolet rays.*

Obvious means easily perceived or understood.
*Our services present **obvious** benefits to your company.*

Oblivious, Forgetful

*See entry for **Forgetful, Oblivious.***

Observance, Observation

Observance refers to the following of a custom, duty, or law.
*The **observance** of Veterans Day varies throughout the state.*

Observation refers to the act of noticing or recording.
*The technician made careful **observations** during the test.*

Obtain, Attain

*See entry for **Attain, Obtain.***

Obtuse, Abstruse

*See entry for **Abstruse, Obtuse.***

Occasional, Intermittent

*See entry for **Intermittent, Occasional.***

Occultist, Oculist

Occultist is one who believes in dark forces, witchcraft, and other supernatural things.
*An **occultist** would usually reject astronomy in favor of astrology.*

Oculist is a physician who treats eyes (synonymous with

ophthalmologist and optometrist).
Oculist Dr. Smith treated my glaucoma.

Octave, Scale

Octave is the distance covered by any eight notes of a scale. A **scale** is a series of eight notes played in alphabetical order.

Odious, Odoriferous, Odorous

Odious means distasteful or offensive.
*Jane thinks cleaning the oven is an **odious** task.*

Odoriferous means having an odor or fragrance.
*Perfume is a blend of certain **odoriferous** substances.*

Odorous refers to something smelly.
*The **odorous** materials need to be placed in plastic bags.*

*The coach was **oblivious** to his star batter's **obvious** bad habits.*

Official

Official, Officious

Official, as an adjective, means authorized or formal. As a noun, it means a person who holds an office.

*Here is an **official** announcement: schools will be closed Friday.*
*The **official** always makes the final ruling.*

Officious means meddling in other people's affairs.

*They opposed any **officious** interference with personal matters.*

Often, Oftentimes

Often is the preferred and simpler word to use.
***Often** (not **oftentimes**) we exercise immediately after work.*

OK, Okay

Avoid these expressions in formal writing.
*We gave our approval (not **OK** or **okay**) to the new project.*

Old-fashion, Old-fashioned

Old-fashioned, meaning outdated, is the correct phrase to use.
*Bob uses an **old-fashioned** approach for teaching applied math.*

Omnipresent, Omniscient

Omnipresent means to be present everywhere simultaneously.
*Technological change is **omnipresent** throughout the world.*

Omniscient means to be all knowing or have total knowledge.
*If he were **omniscient**, he would know how Jenny feels.*

Omnivorous, Carnivorous, Herbivorous

See entry for **Carnivorous, Herbivorous, Omnivorous**.

On route, En route

See entry for **En route, On route**.

On tenderhooks, On tenterhooks

On tenterhooks, meaning to be as tense as the canvas being stretched into a tent, is the correct phrase.

On to, Onto
On to is used when **on** is an adverb and **to** is a preposition.
The engineers then moved on to the next phase of the project.

Onto means to move to a position or to be aware of something.
You can transfer pictures onto your computer in a few steps.
We are onto your plan for restructuring the company.

One and the same, One in the same
One and the same is the correct phrase.

One another, Each other
See entry for Each other, One another.

One of the best, One of the only
Avoid these contradictions. (There can only be one *best* and one *only*, so saying *one of the best* or *only* doesn't make sense.)

Onward, Onwards
Onward is preferred in American usage.

Opaque, Translucent, Transparent
Opaque means no light passes through.
The opaque camera cover protected the film.

Translucent means light passes through, but without clarity.
Translucent bond paper is often used for tracing.

Transparent means light passes through with clarity.
The transparent lid allowed Mom to see the leftovers inside.

Ophthalmologist, Optician, Optometrist
An **ophthalmologist** is an M.D. who specializes in treating eye diseases. An **optician** makes and sells glasses and other optical equipment. An **optometrist** examines one's vision and prescribes eye glasses.

Oppose, Appose
See entry for Appose, Oppose.

Opposite, Apposite
See entry for **Apposite, Opposite**.

Oral, Aural
See entry for **Aural, Oral**.

Oral, Verbal
Oral and **verbal** both refer to things spoken; **verbal** also refers to things written.
*Graduate students are required to do an **oral** report this year.*
*Writer Albert M. Joseph has a **verbal** mastery of our language.*

Ordinal numbers, Cardinal numbers
See entry for **Cardinal numbers, Ordinal numbers**.

Ordinance, Ordnance
Ordinance refers to a decree, law, or regulation.
*Commissioners are discussing an **ordinance** to improve the park.*

Ordnance refers to military equipment or weapons.
*The technology can help find unexploded **ordnance**.*

Ordinary, Common, Mutual, Popular
See entry for **Common, Mutual, Ordinary, Popular**.

Orient, Orientate
Orient is the preferred word.
*We have plenty of time to **orient** ourselves to the project.*

Orthoscopic, Arthroscopic
Arthroscopic is the correct word.
*The surgeon performed **arthroscopic** surgery on his left knee.*

Oscillate, Osculate
Oscillate means to swing back and forth or to be indecisive.
*The speed **oscillated** between 280 rpm and 600 rpm.*
*Her political career **oscillated** between distinction and scandal.*

Osculate means to kiss or touch.
His chief political skill was osculating the infants of voters.

Ostensibly, Ostentatiously

Ostensibly means apparently, evidently, or presumably.
It's a story ostensibly for kids, but more appreciated by adults.

Ostentatiously is an adverb meaning showy or pretentious.
They rarely dress ostentatiously and never flaunt their wealth.

Out loud, Aloud

See entry for Aloud, Out loud.

Jim got a citation for breaking the local ordinance against keeping ordnance in a residence.

Outmost, Upmost, Utmost

Outmost means *outermost* or *farthest out.*
*Jan made a trip to the **outmost** reaches of northern Alaska.*

Upmost is from the word *uppermost* and should not be used in American English.

Utmost means to the greatest degree or intensity.
*Our department treats all information with **utmost** confidentiality.*

Outward, Outwards

Outward is preferred in American usage.

Over, More than

*See entry for **More than, Over**.*

Overlook, Oversee

Overlook means to fail to notice, to disregard, or to ignore.
*We **overlook** the fact that he failed to win the big game.*

Oversee means to direct, supervise, or manage.
*He was hired to **oversee** the operation of the manufacturing site.*

Overt, Covert

*See entry for **Covert, Overt**.*

Overweening, Overwhelming

Overweening means conceited, overbearing, or pretentious.
*We feel his **overweening** ego would not fit with the rest of us.*

Overwhelming means overpowering in effect or strength.
*Doctors feel the artificial heart is an **overwhelming** success.*

P

A good word makes the heart glad. — Proverbs

Palate, Palette, Pallet

Palate is the roof of your mouth.
*A cleft **palate** is a common birth defect.*

Palette is a hand-held board that an artist uses for mixing paint.
*His **palette** contains red, green, and yellow paint.*

Pallet is a flat platform on which goods are loaded.
*Several **pallets** at the warehouse contain new DVD players.*

Palm off, Pawn off

Palm off, meaning to deceive or defraud someone with something inferior, is the correct expression. The phrase probably originated with magicians, who typically use their palms to hide items during tricks.
*They had no right to **palm off** those damaged school buses on the other school districts.*

Paltry, Petty

Paltry means meager, trivial, or measly.
*The company made a **paltry** contribution to the fund this year.*

Petty means minor, trifling, or of little importance.
*The rules apply in **petty** offenses and other misdemeanor cases.*

Pamphlet, Brochure, Leaflet

*See entry for **Brochure, Leaflet, Pamphlet**.*

Parameter, Perimeter

Parameter is a quantity or mathematical variable that stays constant.
*The applet is modified by using the **parameters** in the file.*

Perimeter is the outer boundary of an area.
*The dog never leaves the **perimeter** of the yard.*

Paramount, Tantamount

Paramount means primary or top.
*Customer satisfaction is the **paramount** concern of our staff.*

Tantamount means equivalent to or the same as.
*The general's action is **tantamount** to a declaration of peace.*

Parlay, Parley

Parlay means to bet one's winnings over again. It can also mean to exploit something into something more valuable.
*He **parlayed** his blackjack winnings into enough money to pay for all of his expenses.*
*Using an infomercial, he **parlayed** a simple invention into a national bestseller.*

Parley, as a verb, means to confer with an enemy, to negotiate, or to discuss.
*The leaders plan to **parley** their differences in a neutral location.*

Parley, as a noun, refers to a conference to resolve disagreements or disputes.
*The two leaders agreed to meet for a **parley**.*

Partake, Participate

You **partake** of something and you **participate** in something.
*After **participating** in the tournament, we wanted to **partake** of some refreshments.*

Partially, Partly

Partially means to a certain degree or extent.
*The company **partially** shut down for two weeks to save energy.*

Partly means not completely.
*Doctors feel genetics can be **partly** responsible for mental illness.*

Passable, Passible

Passable means barely satisfactory or able to be passed.
*We sat through a **passable** performance of "Hamlet" last night.*
*Whether the roads are **passable** depends on the weather.*

Passible, a theological term, means capable of feeling or suffering.
*Some believe that God does suffer and is therefore **passible**.*

Passed, Past

Passed is the past tense of *pass.*
*The House and Senate **passed** electronic signature bills.*
*We **passed** that town on the way to St. Louis.*

Past refers to time or distance (and can never be a verb).
*The film covers computer history, from the **past** to the present.*
*We drove **past** that store yesterday.*

Passport, Visa

A **passport** is an official government document that certifies a person's identity and citizenship and permits travel to another country. A **visa** is an official authorization stamped on a passport that permits a person's entry into and travel within a country.

Pastoral, Pastorial

Pastoral is the correct word.

Patience, Patients

Patience refers to the ability to wait.
Patience is a virtue we should all practice.

Patients are people under medical treatment.
*Most **patients** can expect some relief within two to four days.*

Peaceable, Peaceful

Peaceable means inclined to peace.
*The men met in a **peaceable** spirit to resolve their differences.*

Peaceful means tranquil.
*We are committed to making a safe and **peaceful** environment.*

*The climber **piqued** his interest by **peeking** at the mountain **peak** through his telescope.*

Peak, Peek, Pique

Peak, as a noun, means summit; as a verb, it means maximize.
*Those records show Gracie is at the **peak** of her running career.*
*At what age did you **peak** in your running career?*

Peek means to peep or snoop.
***Peek** into the window to see if Karol and Jo have left the house.*

Pique means to excite or irritate.
*Did you **pique** his interest with your sales pitch?*
*After hearing those comments, Ed is definitely **piqued**.*

Peccable, Peccant

Peccable means capable of sinning.
*"A frail and **peccable** mortal"* - Sir Walter Scott.

Peccant means guilty of sinning.
*Opening the skull to relieve **peccant** humors was once common.*

Penultimate, Ultimate

Penultimate means next to last.
*Next week is the **penultimate** week of the fall semester.*

Ultimate means last or superlative.
*The **ultimate** fate of Atlantis is unknown.*
*Mary prepared the **ultimate** apple pie for my birthday.*

People, Persons

People and **persons** are generally interchangeable, but **people** is the preferred word. **Persons** may be considered overly formal or haughty.

Per say, Per se

Per se, meaning *as such* or *intrinsically*, is the correct phrase.
*Partisanship **per se** does not preclude political action.*

Percent, Percentage, Percentage point

Percent is specific and is usually used with a number.
*They expect to reduce their workforce by 15 **percent**.*

Percentage is not specific and is never used with a number.
*The reduction affects a small **percentage** of engineers.*

Note: **Percent** should be spelled as one word (not **per cent**).
Also, **percent** is becoming accepted without a number by it.
*What **percent** of your workday is spent in meetings?*

Percentage point is the correct phrase when referring to a change in a figure that is already a percentage. One percentage point is always 1/100th of the total.
*The President's approval rating fell from 43 percent to 40 percent, a drop of three **percentage points** (not 3 percent).*

Perfume, Cologne

*See entry for **Cologne, Perfume**.*

Periodic, Sporadic

Periodic means occurring at regular or predictable intervals.
*Lisa told us she would be having **periodic** performance reviews.*

Sporadic means occurring at irregular or unpredictable times.
*Some western states are experiencing **sporadic** power outages.*

Perpetrate, Perpetuate

Perpetrate means being responsible for something.
*Bill likes to **perpetrate** practical jokes on his teammates.*

Perpetuate means cause to be remembered or last indefinitely.
*The Vietnam Memorial **perpetuates** the memory of those killed in that war.*

Perquisite, Prerequisite

Perquisite refers to a special benefit or privilege (a **perq**).
*A new company car is a **perquisite** for all their executives.*

Prerequisite refers to something required in advance.
*What **prerequisite** course does the college require for admission to this program?*

Persecute, Prosecute

Persecute means to harass or treat unjustly.
*The committee may **persecute** them for their political dissent.*

Prosecute means to bring legal action against or to pursue something until the end.
*Some states **prosecute** juveniles as adults in criminal court.*
*Their patent **prosecution** on DNA techniques helped the industry.*

Person that, Person who

Person who is the preferred phrase in formal writing. Some purists reserve **who** for people and **that** for animals or things.
*Jeff is the **person who** chose engineering as a career.*
*That's the elephant **that** almost lost its memory.*

Personal, Personnel
Personal means private.
*My date did not want to discuss **personal** matters.*

Personnel means a group of people, usually all of whom are part of the same organization.
*We have the qualified **personnel** to get the job done.*
*The **Personnel** Department handles the employee's exit interview.*

Perspective, Prospective
Perspective is a point of view or a way to create the illusion of depth in a drawing or painting.
*From the teacher's **perspective**, it is another way of learning.*
*The painting shows a three-dimensional **perspective** of Toronto.*

Prospective means probable.
*The **prospective** buyer went to the web site to learn more.*

Perspicacious, Perspicuous
Perspicacious means having a quick understanding of things.
*Anand is a **perspicacious** student of law.*

Perspicuous means presenting things clearly and precisely.
*Their account of the events is quite **perspicuous** to everyone.*

Persuade, Convince
*See entry for **Convince, Persuade**.*

Peruse, Skim
Peruse means to examine or read carefully.
*They want to **peruse** the contract thoroughly before signing it.*

Skim means glance over or read quickly.
*He intended to **skim** the material right before the meeting.*

Perverbial, Proverbial
Proverbial is the correct word.

Phase

*From the **prospective** student's **perspective**, the rowdy campus looked great.*

Phase, Faze
*See entry for **Faze, Phase**.*

Phenomena, Phenomenon
Phenomena is the plural form of the noun **phenomenon**.
*Such **phenomena** are difficult to comprehend and explain.*
*Many sightings continue to fuel the UFO **phenomenon**.*

Philippinos, Filipinos

People of the Philippines are referred to as **Filipinos**.

Physician, Doctor

*See entry for **Doctor, Physician**.*

Picaresque, Picturesque

Picaresque refers to adventurers or clever rogues.
*Twain's "Tom Sawyer" contains many **picaresque** characters.*

Picturesque refers to being attractive or pretty.
*Lake Placid contains some wonderful **picturesque** views.*

Pitfall, Pratfall

A **pitfall** is an unexpected danger.
*The mercenary encountered many **pitfalls** while fighting rebels.*

A **pratfall** is a comical or humiliating fall, often used in physical humor.
*The kindergartners laughed uproariously at the clown's **pratfalls**.*

Plaintiff, Plaintive

Plaintiff refers to one who brings a suit into a court of law.
*The **plaintiff** claimed the defendant scratched his new Mercedes.*

Plaintive refers to being mournful or melancholy.
*A **plaintive** cry for help could be heard in the distance.*

Plan on, Plan to

Plan to is the preferred phrase.
*Please **plan to** attend our next chapter meeting.*

Plaque, Tartar

Plaque is a thin film of mucus and bacteria on a tooth's surface.
Tartar (also called dental calculus) is a hard, yellowish plaque that collects food particles and salt deposits.

Playwright, Playwrite

Someone who writes plays is a **playwright**, not a **playwrite**.

Plenitude, Plentitude

Plenitude is preferred in American usage.

Plethora, Dearth

See entry for ***Dearth, Plethora****.*

Plum, Plumb

Plum is the juicy fruit.
*In the summer, I could eat **plums** all day.*

Plumb means to explore something fully.
*He **plumbed** the depths of inner-city life for his new novel.*

Plurality, Majority

See entry for ***Majority, Plurality****.*

Podium, Lectern, Rostrum

See entry for ***Lectern, Podium, Rostrum****.*

Pom-pom, Pompon

Pom-pom is a lightweight, automatic cannon. **Pompon** is what a cheerleader waves.

Populace, Populous

Populace, a noun, refers to the common people or population.
*The city of Los Angeles has a huge and growing **populace**.*

Populous, an adjective, means densely populated.
*San Diego is a **populous** and growing southern California city.*

Popular, Common, Mutual, Ordinary

See entry for ***Common, Mutual, Ordinary, Popular****.*

Port, Harbor

See entry for ***Harbor, Port****.*

Portend, Pretend

Portend means to indicate beforehand.
*An increase in downsizing could **portend** a tough job market.*

Pretend means to make believe, profess, or disguise.
*Children like to **pretend** sometimes that they are adults.*

Portion, Apportion, Proportion

*See entry for **Apportion, Portion, Proportion**.*

Possible, Probable

Possible means it could happen or be done.
*It's **possible** the hurricane could hit New York by next week.*

Probable means it is likely to happen.
*It's **probable** the hurricane will hit the Carolina coast today.*

Postpone, Cancel, Delay

*See entry for **Cancel, Delay, Postpone**.*

Practicable, Practical

Practicable means capable of being put into practice.
*Considering the budget, is it **practicable** to build a new arena?*

Practical means useful, sensible, or worth being put into practice.
*The plan contains **practical** measures for improving traffic flow.*

Pragmatic, Dogmatic

*See entry for **Dogmatic, Pragmatic**.*

Precede, Proceed

Precede means to go before something.
*The national anthem **precedes** all of our baseball games.*

Proceed means to go ahead with an action.
*Click here if you wish to **proceed** to the next step.*

Precedence, Precedents

Precedence refers to priority, rank, or an act of coming before.
The need for safety took **precedence** *over all other matters.*

Precedents refers to previous actions that serve as examples.
A few decisions established **precedents** *for the pursuit of justice.*

Precipitate, Precipitous

Precipitate, as an adjective, means rash or sudden.
Their **precipitate** *entry into the dot com market led to a disaster.*

Precipitous means very steep.
Video conferencing is leading to a **precipitous** *decline in travel.*

Predominant, Predominate

Predominant, an adjective, means the most common or conspicuous.
The **predominant** *view is that he is the best athlete ever.*

Predominate, a verb, means to prevail or wield greater power or quantity.
The good will of the people definitely **predominates** *in this town.*

Note: Older dictionaries list the words as synonyms if used as adjectives.

Preface, Foreword, Introduction

See entry for **Foreword, Introduction, Preface.**

Premature, Immature

See entry for **Immature, Premature.**

Premier, Premiere

Premier, as an adjective, means first in importance. As a noun, it means a chief government executive.
That is one of the **premier** *magazines on the newsstands today.*
The **premier** *of that country invited us to his palace for dinner.*

Premiere means opening night or first public showing.
We attended the **premiere** *of "The Phantom of the Opera."*

Premise, Premises

Premise refers to an assumption or a supposition.
He understands the basic premise of public relations.

Premises refers to a house, building, grounds, or other property.
Finding the right office premises may improve productivity.

Prescribe, Proscribe

Prescribe means to set down a rule or to order something.
The labor law prescribes a standard 40-hour workweek.
Perhaps the doctor can prescribe a more effective drug.

Proscribe means to condemn, forbid, or prohibit something.
The Food and Drug Administration proscribed Laetrile years ago.

Presentiment, Presentment

Presentiment means premonition.
The studio has a presentiment that the film will be a success.

A **presentment** is something exhibited or presented.
She reimburses you upon presentment of a signed receipt.

Press, Click, Type

See entry for Click, Press, Type.

Presume, Assume

See entry for Assume, Presume.

Presumptive, Presumptuous

Presumptive means presumed.
Smith is the presumptive new CEO, though he hasn't been promoted yet.

Presumptuous means arrogant, bold, or forward.
It is presumptuous of them to invite themselves to our party.

Pretense, Pretext

Pretense is a false claim or a show of insincere behavior.
*The drug should not be legalized under any **pretense**.*
*The compliments we received were all **pretense**.*

Pretext is the professed purpose for something, usually false.
*Mark lost his job under the **pretext** of being overqualified.*

Prevaricate, Procrastinate, Equivocate

*See entry for **Equivocate, Prevaricate, Procrastinate**.*

Preventative, Preventive

Preventive is the preferred spelling, but either is acceptable.
***Preventive** dentistry measures can lead to healthier smiles.*

Principal, Principle

Principal, as an adjective, means foremost. As a noun, it is the head of a school or the amount of money borrowed.
*Who are the **principal** developers of the new hardware product?*
*The middle school is getting a new **principal** for the fall.*
*The mortgage payment includes both **principal** and interest.*

Principle is a noun that refers to law or personal conviction.
*It works on the **principle** that warm air rises.*
*It is against our basic **principles** to make such a statement.*

Prison, Jail

*See entry for **Jail, Prison**.*

Problem, Dilemma

*See entry for **Dilemma, Problem**.*

Problematic, Problemsome

Problematic is the correct word.

Procrastinate, Equivocate, Prevaricate

*See entry for **Equivocate, Prevaricate, Procrastinate**.*

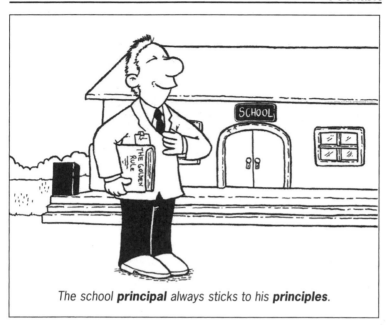

*The school **principal** always sticks to his **principles**.*

Prodigy, Protégé, Protégée

Prodigy refers to a person with exceptional talents.
*Many musicians considered Mozart a child **prodigy**.*

Protégé is a male who is guided or helped by someone.
*As a youth, Justin considered himself a **protégé** of Buddy Holly.*

Protégée is a female who is guided or helped by someone.
*Loretta was a **protégée** of Jane, the head accountant.*

Prognosis, Diagnosis

*See entry for **Diagnosis, Prognosis**.*

Prohibit, Forbid

*See entry for **Forbid, Prohibit**.*

Prone, Prostrate, Supine

Prone means lying face down.
*The old man enjoys sleeping in the **prone** position.*

Prostrate also means lying face down (often after an accident).
*The football player lies **prostrate** after the tackle.*

Supine means lying face up.
*The beach is full of sun worshippers, **supine** on the sand.*

Proof, Evidence

*See entry for **Evidence, Proof**.*

Prophecy, Prophesy

Prophecy, a noun, means a prediction.
*Is there a **prophecy** in that book that could be fulfilled this year?*

Prophesy, a verb, means to predict by divine inspiration.
*What did they **prophesy** about our future on Earth?*

Proportion, Apportion, Portion

*See entry for **Apportion, Portion, Proportion**.*

Protagonist, Antagonist

*See entry for **Antagonist, Protagonist**.*

Protean, Protein

Protean means versatile or capable of taking on varied shapes or meanings.
*Robert De Niro has shown his **protean** talent in many films.*

Protein is an organic compound essential for living cells.
*Nutritionists say high-**protein** diets may pose a risk to health.*

Proved, Proven

Proved, a verb, means to establish the truth of something.
*Inconsistencies in the man's testimony **proved** he was lying.*

Proven, a past participle of *prove*, is used only as an adjective.
*Hypnosis is a **proven** and popular method for quitting smoking.*

Prudent, Prudish

Prudent means exercising good common sense or judgment.
*It was **prudent** of them to invest in the company when they did.*

Prudish means very formal, precise, or reserved.
*Our company is too **prudish** to introduce a relaxed dress code.*

Pseudo, Quasi

Pseudo is a prefix meaning false, counterfeit, or deceptive. It requires a hyphen when joined to a proper noun.
*The **pseudo**science didn't impress the potential investors.*
*The **pseudo**-European furniture, made in China, sold well.*

Quasi is a prefix meaning resembling or *in some manner*. It is usually hyphenated.
*The **quasi** scientific literature presented little bona fide research.*

Purposefully, Purposely

Purposefully means to act with determination or purpose.
*The coach strode **purposefully** to the TV booth for an interview.*

Purposely means to do something deliberately or intentionally.
*Please do not remove those books — I put them there **purposely**.*

Q

One should not aim at being possible to understand, but at being impossible to misunderstand.

– Quintillian

Qualitative, Quantitative

Qualitative refers to the characteristics or properties of quality, and **quantitative** refers to the measure of something.
Qualitative data is information that is not clearly quantifiable, such as a scientist's observations, the taste of something, or a videotape of an interview. **Quantitative** data can be counted, such as the temperature of a liquid, the number of petals on a flower, or the amount of salt in a gallon of seawater.

Quash, Squash

Quash, which typically refers to legal action, means to annul or invalidate.
*Censorship rules permit authorities to **quash** almost anything.*

Squash means to crush, squeeze, or suppress.
*If they had aspirations of winning, their hopes were **squashed**.*

Quasi, Pseudo

*See entry for **Pseudo, Quasi**.*

Queue, Cue

*See entry for **Cue, Queue**.*

Quiet, Quite

Quiet means silence.
*"All **Quiet** on the Western Front" was the first antiwar film with sound.*

Quite means really or close.
*The banana could **quite** possibly be the world's perfect food.*
*Jeb wasn't **quite** the right person for this assignment.*

Quotation, Quote

Quotation, a noun, refers to words somebody said.
*The **quotations** of JFK and Churchill continue to be popular.*

Quote, a verb, means to repeat the words of someone.
*Do you mind if the press **quotes** you on that statement?*

Note: Used informally, **quote** is the shortened word for **quotation**.
*That movie has many memorable **quotes**.*

R

Scarcely any of our intellectual operations could be carried on to any considerable extent without the agency of words.

– Peter Roget

Rabble rouser, Rebel rouser

Rabble rouser, an agitator, is the correct expression. The phrase first appeared in England in the mid-19th century as a combination of *rabble* and *rouse*.
A group of **rabble rousers** *disrupted the football game.*

Rack, Wrack

Rack and **wrack** both mean to strain or torment. Prefer **rack**.
We are **racking** *our brains to remember the name of that song.*

Rancor, Ranker

Rancor refers to long-lasting bitterness or hatred.
The explosive testimony brought even more courtroom **rancor**.

Ranker refers to a person with an official position or grade.
The paper says he was only a middle **ranker** *and not a senior military leader.*

Rarely ever

Avoid this phrase. Just use **rarely** by itself.
Rarely (not **rarely ever***) do we hire someone without a degree.*

Raucous, Ruckus

Raucous, an adjective, means loud or rambunctious.
It was not unusual for them to throw a **raucous** *party after a game.*

Ruckus, a noun, means a fight, disturbance, or commotion.
The authorities are more interested in stopping the **ruckus** *than in figuring out who started it.*

Ravage, Ravish

Ravage means to destroy or devastate something.
*Fires continued to **ravage** the western states for many weeks.*

Ravish means to carry off by force or overwhelm with emotion.
*In the novel, the king's daughter was **ravished** by her captors.*
*The beauty of the Canadian sunset **ravished** the travelers.*

Rebound, Redound

Rebound means to bounce or spring back.
*The company's stock price **rebounded** after the news hit.*

Redound means to contribute or lead to something.
*Her exceptional performance **redounds** to the company's benefit.*

Rebuff, Rebut, Refute, Repudiate

Rebuff means to snub or reject someone.
*We offered to help with the cleanup, but he **rebuffed** us.*

Rebut means to argue against something.
*Unless the board **rebuts** the proposal, the idea is accepted.*

Refute means to prove something is false.
*The defense team was able to **refute** much of the testimony.*

Repudiate means to reject or refuse something.
*We were always taught to **repudiate** discrimination and violence.*

Recapitulate, Capitulate

See entry for **Capitulate, Recapitulate**.

Recital, Concert

See entry for **Concert, Recital**.

Recourse

Recourse, Resort

Recourse refers to turning to someone or something for help.
*What **recourse** do online shoppers have today?*

Resort, as a noun, is something you turn to after all other options have failed. **Resort**, as a verb, means to have recourse.
*As a last **resort**, I contacted the police.*
*Because of the accident, he had to **resort** to riding his bike.*

Recur, Reoccur

Recur is the preferred word.

Reeking havoc, Wreaking havoc

Wreaking havoc is the correct phrase.
*The power surges are **wreaking havoc** with our new computer.*

Refer, Allude, Elude

*See entry for **Allude, Elude, Refer**.*

Refrain, Restrain

Refrain means to choose not to do something or partake of something.
*The students were asked to **refrain** from leaving class early.*

Restrain means to immobilize by force or to forbid an action.
*The nurses had to **restrain** the patient in order to avoid injury.*

Regardless, Irregardless

*See entry for **Irregardless, Regardless**.*

Regime, Regimen, Regiment

Regime, a noun, refers to a government, usually an authoritarian one.
*The country underwent **regime** change on its own terms.*

Regimen, a noun, refers to a therapeutic treatment, usually including diet and exercise.
*The benefits of a daily fitness **regimen** are endless.*

Regiment, as a noun, refers to a military unit or large group of people; as a verb, it means to direct or command.
*The people's good wishes went to the soldiers of our **regiment**.*
*They sought to **regiment** the people and their property.*

Regretfully, Regrettably

Regretfully means with feelings of regret.
*Prior commitments made him **regretfully** decline the invitation.*

Regrettably means unfortunately.
*It looked like the rain would stop, but **regrettably** it did not.*

Reknown, Renown

Renown, meaning fame, is the correct word. **Reknown** is not a word.

Relegate, Delegate

*See entry for **Delegate, Relegate**.*

Reluctant, Reticent

Reluctant means opposing or unwilling to act.
*Few golfers are **reluctant** to wear soft spikes on the course.*

Reticent means keeping silent or unwilling to speak freely.
*Her **reticent** nature conceals many of her talents.*

Remarkable, Marked

*See entry for **Marked, Remarkable**.*

Remediable, Remedial

Remediable means capable of being corrected or remedied.
*Dr. Watson assures us your teeth problems are **remediable**.*

Remedial means supplying a remedy.
*A research brief on **remedial** education is available at the office.*

Renounce, Denounce

*See entry for **Denounce, Renounce**.*

Repertoire

Repertoire, Repertory

Repertoire is the range of entertainment a person or group performs.
*Larry has a good **repertoire** of corny jokes that we enjoy.*

Repertory is the place where a person or group performs.
*The Owego Drama Players have their own **repertory** theatre.*

Represented, Representated

Representated is not a word.

Reputation, Character

*See entry for **Character, Reputation**.*

Request, Behest

*See entry for **Behest, Request**.*

Resident, Citizen

*See entry for **Citizen, Resident**.*

Resister, Resistor

Resister is anyone who offers resistance. **Resistor** is a device that controls current in an electrical circuit.

Respectably, Respectfully, Respectively

Respectably means in a decent way.
*All of the invitees are dressed **respectably** for the occasion.*

Respectfully means in a courteous way.
*Tom **respectfully** submitted his opinion to the city council.*

Respectively means in the order given or indicated.
*Harold and Ted are an engineer and lawyer, **respectively**.*

Restive, Restless

Restive means impatient or fidgety under pressure or restraint.
*The guards are worried about the **restive** prisoners.*

Restless means uneasy, unquiet, or unable to rest or relax.
*The doctor felt her **restless** nights were due to sleep apnea.*

Retch, Wretch

Retch refers to vomiting or gagging; **wretch** refers to a pitiable or groveling person.

Retroactive from, Retroactive to

Retroactive to is the preferred phrase.
*The salary increases are **retroactive to** January 1.*

Revolve, Rotate

These words are synonyms in everyday writing but not in scientific or technical writing.
*The earth **revolves** around the sun and **rotates** upon its axis.*

Reward, Award

*See entry for **Award, Reward**.*

Riffle, Rifle

Riffle means to browse or thumb through something.
*She **riffled** the class material just before the test.*

Rifle means to ransack or steal something.
*Someone **rifled** through their house while they were out of town.*

Right, Wright

Right means morally, legally, or properly.
*The umpire did the **right** thing when he admitted his mistake.*

Wright is a maker such as a playwright.
*Many people consider Neil Simon a famous American **wright**.*

Rightfully, Rightly

Rightfully means having a claim or right to something.
*Marty is **rightfully** the owner of the rare painting.*

Rightly means correctly or properly.
*Joe **rightly** refuses to sign a contract until an accord is reached.*

Rigorous, Vigorous

Rigorous means harsh, precise, severe, or strict.
*The senior class underwent a **rigorous** training course.*

Vigorous means energetic, robust, or strong.
*Some dentists say teeth do not need **vigorous** brushing.*

Robbery, Burglary, Theft

See entry for **Burglary, Robbery, Theft.**

Rostrum, Lectern, Podium

See entry for **Lectern, Podium, Rostrum.**

S

My words fly up, my thoughts remain below: Words without thoughts never to heaven go.

– William Shakespeare

Sachet, Sashay

Sachet is a small packet of perfumed powder.
*While drying her clothes, Lois dropped a small **sachet** in the dryer.*

Sashay means to strut or flounce.
*After their victory, the girls proudly **sashayed** around the field.*

Safe-deposit box, Safety deposit box
Safe-deposit box is the correct phrase.

Salacious, Salubrious
Salacious means lecherous, lustful, or obscene.
*We all receive **salacious**, virus-bearing e-mail.*

Salubrious means conducive or favorable to health and well-being.
*Every winter they enjoy the **salubrious** weather in Florida.*

Salon, Saloon
A **salon** is a large room usually used for entertaining people, cutting hair, or exhibiting artwork. A **saloon** is a place where alcoholic beverages are sold.

Sanguinary, Sanguine
Sanguinary means bloody or murderous.
*The Battle of Gettysburg was the most **sanguinary** battle ever fought on this continent.*

Sanguine means cheerful, optimistic, or confident.
*She is **sanguine** about the future and happy to have a new job.*

197

Sarcastic

Sarcastic, Skeptical, Cynical
See entry for **Cynical, Sarcastic, Skeptical**.

Saving, Savings
Saving refers to something preserved.
*With the new process, we realized a **saving** of two hours.*

Use **savings** when referring to banks, bank accounts, and bonds.
*We opened a **savings** account that yields a high interest rate.*
*John won a $100 **savings** bond in the speech contest.*

Note: One would never write, "a losses of $20," so one should not write, "a savings of $20."
*The girl invested her **saving** of $500 in a **savings** bond.*

Scale, Octave
See entry for **Octave, Scale**.

Scapegoat, Escape goat
See entry for **Escape goat, Scapegoat**.

Schilling, Shilling
Schilling is Austrian currency and **shilling** is British currency.

Scrupulous, Meticulous
See entry for **Meticulous, Scrupulous**.

Scull, Skull
Scull is an oar used by a rower.
*Dan and Ben are propelling their new canoe with heavy **sculls**.*

Skull is the bone that protects the brain and face.
*You can get a slight **skull** fracture and sometimes not realize it.*

Seasonable, Seasonal

Seasonable means appropriate for the season or occasion.
*The sleet is unexpected but **seasonable** for this time of year.*

Seasonal refers to a particular season.
*Her **seasonal** work includes giving golf lessons in Miami.*

Sectarian, Secular

Sectarian refers to sects or religious groups.
*His message was a **sectarian** appeal to help others get funding.*

Secular means not connected to a religion.
*Although identified as a **secular** charity, it will get some donations from the church.*

Seeing as, Seeing that

Avoid these phrases in writing. Use *because* instead.
*Because (not **seeing as** or **seeing that**) our car broke down, we missed our starting time.*

*Fred knew they were in trouble when his **scull** hit a **skull**.*

Seize the day, Cease the day
Seize the day is the correct phrase.

Semiannual
Synonym for *biannual* (twice a year). *See entry for **Biannual, Biennial**.*

Semimonthly, Bimonthly
*See entry for **Bimonthly, Semimonthly**.*

Sensual, Sensuous
Sensual means physically gratifying to the body or its senses.
*She delighted in the **sensual** warmth of the Hawaiian Islands.*

Sensuous means appealing to the senses.
*Her music is not only warm and **sensuous**, but relaxing as well.*

Session, Cession
*See entry for **Cession, Session**.*

Shade, Hue, Tint
*See entry for **Hue, Shade, Tint**.*

Shall, Will
Today in everyday American business writing and speaking, the **wills** outnumber the **shalls**. Few people distinguish between them anymore. But if you are a traditionalist, here are the rules for handling **shall** and **will**:

Shall is used for the first-person future tense.
*We **shall** enjoy working for the new town supervisor.*

Will is used for the second and third-person future tense.
*You (They) **will** enjoy working for the new town supervisor.*

For legal documents and some government contracts, **shall** expresses determination or a guarantee, and **will** expresses a plan to do something. Either word can be used with first-, second-, or third-person pronouns in the future tense.

We (You, They) **shall** supply the required documentation when requested by the customer.
Before the end of the month, the supervisor **will** appraise all of her employees.

Shanty, Chantey
See entry for **Chantey, Shanty**.

Sherbet, Sherbert, Sorbet
Use **sherbet** (with one *r*), not **sherbert**, when referring to the ice cream-like confection. **Sorbet** is a fancy restaurant's **sherbet**.

Should have, Should of
Should have is the correct phrase.
They **should have** come downstairs earlier.

Shudder, Shutter
Shudder means to vibrate, shake, or shiver from fear, revulsion, or cold.
The severe air turbulence caused the airplane to **shudder**.
I **shudder** to imagine where we will be if the measure fails.

Shutter is a screen or cover, or a moveable cover for a window.
A camera's **shutter** is similar to a person's eyelid.
Jill closed the window **shutters** during the storm.

Shudder to think, Shutter to think
Shudder to think is the correct expression.

Sight, Site, Cite
See entry for **Cite, Sight, Site**.

Silicon, Silicone
Silicon is the nonmetallic chemical element used in microchips.
The technician put the **silicon** wafer into the slot.

Silicone is plastic and other materials that contain silicon.
Silicone is widely used as a protective coating for shoes.

Simple, Simplistic

Simple means plain, not complex, or uncomplicated.
*Joe's explanation is quite **simple** and easy to comprehend.*

Simplistic means unrealistically simple and is usually used in a derogatory sense.
*Bob's explanation is quite **simplistic** and omits many key points.*

Simulate, Emulate

*See entry for **Emulate, Simulate**.*

*Jessica **shuddered** by the open **shutters**.*

Sinecure, Cynosure
See entry for **Cynosure, Sinecure**.

Sister-in-laws, Sisters-in-law
Sisters-in-law is the correct phrase.

Site, Cite, Sight
See entry for **Cite, Sight, Site**.

Skeptical, Cynical, Sarcastic
See entry for **Cynical, Sarcastic, Skeptical**.

Sketch, Skit
Though both are short, entertaining presentations, a **sketch** is usually serious and unrehearsed while a **skit** is typically rehearsed and comical.

Skiddish, Skittish
Skittish is the correct word.

Skim, Peruse
See entry for **Peruse, Skim**.

Slander, Liable, Libel, Lible
See entry for **Liable, Libel, Lible, Slander**.

Slither of cake, Sliver of cake
Sliver of cake is the correct expression.

Slogan, Motto
See entry for **Motto, Slogan**.

Solid, Stolid

Solid means reliable when referring to a person's character.
*He has a reputation as a **solid** citizen.*

Stolid means unemotional or stoic.
*The funny entertainer could even make a **stolid** person let loose.*

Some time, Sometime, Sometimes

Some time means a period of time.
*Gordon needs **some time** to think over the attractive job offer.*

Sometime refers to an indefinite time in the future.
*Let's try to get together and have lunch **sometime**.*

Sometimes means now and then.
*Tim likes golf a lot, but **sometimes** he needs to give it a rest.*

Somewhere, Somewheres

Somewhere is the correct word.
***Somewhere** out in deep space, our planet might have a twin.*

Son-in-laws, Sons-in-law

Sons-in-law is the correct phrase.

Sordid story, Sorted story

Sordid story is the correct phrase.

Sort of, Kind of

*See entry for **Kind of, Sort of**.*

Southward, Southwards

Southward is preferred in American usage.

Spacious, Specious

Spacious means roomy or large in area.
*The hotel offers **spacious** accommodations at affordable rates.*

Specious means plausible but false.
*He is known for using **specious** arguments to back his claims.*

Spade, Spayed

Spade is a small digging tool.
The soil in our garden can be turned by hand with a **spade**.

A **spayed** female animal has had its ovaries removed.
Spayed *cats are typically affectionate, calm, and healthy.*

Specially, Especially

See entry for **Especially, Specially***.*

Specie, Species

Concerning classification in biology, **species** is the correct spelling for both singular and plural.
This (or those) **species** *may soon be extinct.*

Spiritual, Spirituous

Spiritual refers to the spirit or soul.
Friends can offer comfort, empathy, and **spiritual** *support.*

Spirituous refers to certain kinds of alcoholic drinks.
The city allows the sale of **spirituous** *liquors in sealed containers.*

Spoor, Spore

Spoor is the track or trail of an animal.
The hunters are tracking the deer in the snow by its **spoor***.*

Spore is the reproductive organ of a fern, algae, and some other plant-like organisms.
You can see the **spores** *under the leaves of the fern.*

Sporadic, Periodic

See entry for **Periodic, Sporadic***.*

Squash, Quash

See entry for **Quash, Squash***.*

Stain glass, Stained glass

Stained glass is the correct phrase.

Stalactites, Stalagmites

Both words refer to crystalline deposits of calcium carbonate found in caves. **Stalactites** hang from the ceiling, and **stalagmites** rise from the ground.

Stanch, Staunch

Stanch means to block something.
*They're allocating a lot money to **stanch** the flow of illegal drugs.*

Staunch means dedicated or loyal. **Staunch** can also mean watertight or sound (a **staunch** ship).
*Bob is always a **staunch** supporter of that political party.*

Stanza, Verse

Technically, a **stanza** is a succession of lines that form a poem or a song. **Verse** is a single line of writing. However, we also call a series of lines in a song a **verse**.

Stationary, Stationery

Stationary means unable to move or to stand still.
***Stationary** bikes offer a great cardio lower-body workout.*

Stationery is paper for letter writing.
*Creating personalized business **stationery** is easy.*

Statue, Stature, Statute

Statue is a sculpture that represents a human or animal.
*With the base and pedestal, the **Statue** of Liberty is 305 feet tall.*

Stature refers to height or status.
*The child could have a genetic short **stature** or a growth delay.*
*Their software company grew in **stature** in just a few years.*

Statute is an established law or rule.
*The city's **statute** of limitations limits the time for tax collection.*

"A city **statute** prohibits a **statue** of this **stature**," the inspector told the sculptor.

Stimulant

Stimulant, Stimulus

Stimulant refers to drugs or other things that increase activity.
*Caffeine, a mild **stimulant**, acts on the central nervous system.*

Stimulus refers to an incentive that initiates activity.
*Music alone can provide a **stimulus** to a person's imagination.*

Straight, Strait

Straight means not curved.
*Unlike many rivers, the Hudson River runs **straight** for one mile.*

Strait, as an adjective, means confined or restricted. As a noun, it means a narrow passage.
*He is a pretty **strait**-laced type of person with high principles.*
*The **Strait** of Hormuz is the entrance to the Persian Gulf.*

Stupid, Ignorant

*See entry for **Ignorant, Stupid**.*

Subnormal, Abnormal

*See entry for **Abnormal, Subnormal**.*

Subscribe, Ascribe

*See entry for **Ascribe, Subscribe**.*

Subsequent, Consequent

*See entry for **Consequent, Subsequent**.*

Substantial, Substantive

Substantial means considerable or sizeable.
*We need a **substantial** revenue increase to meet our goals.*

Substantive means actual or firm.
*The boss is taking **substantive** measures to prevent layoffs.*

Supercede, Supersede

The preferred spelling is **supersede**.

Supine, Prone, Prostrate
See entry for **Prone, Prostrate, Supine.**

Supplement, Augment
See entry for **Augment, Supplement.**

Supposably, Supposedly
Though both words can be found in dictionaries and are close in meaning, the preferred word is **supposedly**.
*They **supposedly** saved the toughest questions for the end.*

Suppose, Supposed
Suppose, a verb, means to think or guess.
***Suppose** we win the lottery next week. What are we buying first?*

Supposed, an adjective, means accepted as such or believed, but often with a doubtful connotation.
*His **supposed** expertise didn't impress the computer programmers who had worked with his software.*

Suppose to, Supposed to
Supposed to is the correct phrase.
*What is **supposed to** be so special about this design software?*

Sure, Surely
Sure is an adjective.
*Waiting for hours is a **sure** sign of his patience and dedication.*

Surely is an adverb.
*Waiting for hours is **surely** a sign of his patience and dedication.*

Note: Careful writers try to avoid using the following informal uses of **sure**:
***Sure** enough, I'll be there.*
*She **sure** is a nice person.*
*He **sure** needed the money.*
***Sure**, I want to attend college.*

Sure and, Sure to

Sure to is the correct phrase.
*Be **sure to** negotiate beneficial compromises for all of your clients.*

Sympathy, Empathy

*See entry for **Empathy, Sympathy**.*

Syntax, Grammar

*See entry for **Grammar, Syntax**.*

Systematize, Systemize

Systematize is the preferred spelling, but either is acceptable.

T

T–shirt, Tee shirt
Either spelling is acceptable.

Take, Bring
*See entry for **Bring, Take**.*

Take a different tack, Take a different tact
Take a different tack is the correct phrase. It means to take a different strategy, and it derives from the nautical term *tack*, which is a ship's direction in relation to the position of its sails. *We're going **to take a different tack** this year and focus on quality.*

Tantamount, Paramount
*See entry for **Paramount, Tantamount**.*

Tartar, Plaque
*See entry for **Plaque, Tartar**.*

Taunt, Taut
Taunt means to jeer, mock, scoff, or tease someone. *Frank confronted the person who **taunted** him during his speech.*

Taut means tightly stretched or tense. *For safety reasons, the rope is kept **taut** for the rock climbers.*

Teach, Learn
*See entry for **Learn, Teach**.*

Temerity, Timidity

Temerity means daring or recklessness.
*Nick had the **temerity** to ask the film star for another autograph.*

Timidity means fearfulness or hesitancy.
__Timidity__ and shyness are common to many young children.

Temperature, Fever

*See entry for **Fever, Temperature**.*

Tenant, Tenet

Tenant refers to one who holds the right (or lease) to occupy a place.
*The previous **tenant** of this apartment lived here for 12 years.*

Tenet refers to a rule, belief, or part of a body of doctrine.
*Avoiding pork altogether is a **tenet** of some faiths.*

Tendon, Ligament

*See entry for **Ligament, Tendon**.*

That there, Them there, These here, This here

Avoid these phrases. Just use **that**, **those**, **these**, or **this**.

That, Which

That is used when the word introduces a clause essential (or restrictive) to the meaning of the sentence. **That** helps identify the information and is not set off by commas.
*This is the Chevy **that** has a new engine.*
*Here is the rule **that** applies in both cases.*

Which is used when the word introduces a clause not essential (or nonrestrictive) to the meaning of the sentence. **Which** helps amplify the information and is set off by commas or dashes.
*My Chevy, **which** runs well, has a new engine.*
*This rule, **which** became effective in 2002, applies to you.*

Memory hook: **That** identifies and **which** amplifies.

Thaw, Unthaw
Thaw is the correct word. The *un* is unnecessary.

Theft, Burglary, Robbery
See entry for **Burglary, Robbery, Theft.**

Their, There, They're
Their is the possessive of the pronoun *they;* **there** is an adverb or a pronoun referring to a place; **they're** is the contraction of *they are.*
*They're doing all **their** science homework over **there** tonight.*

Theirself, Theirselves, Themself
No such words exist. Substitute *herself* or *himself* for **theirself** and *themselves* for **theirselves** and **themself.**

Thence, Hence, Whence
See entry for **Hence, Thence, Whence.**

Therefor, Therefore
Therefor, a rare word, means *for this* or *for that.*
*John will explain what we must do first and the causes **therefor.***

Therefore means hence or consequently.
*We **therefore** hold that the two-week notice is too short.*

These kind, Those kind
Avoid these phrases because they mix a plural word (*these* or *those*) with a singular word (*kind*). Instead, use *this kind* and *that kind*, or *these kinds* and *those kinds*.

Note that this agreement problem can also occur with the phrases *these sort* and *these type*.

These ones, Those ones
Avoid these phrases. Just use *these* or *those*.

Thrash

Thrash, Thresh

Thrash means to beat, defeat, or move violently.
*In yesterday's ballgame, we **thrashed** the Astros.*
*Some in the yoga class **thrashed** their arms about like windmills.*

Thresh means to separate seeds of grain from husks by beating.
*The farm workers **thresh** the wheat in the fields twice a week.*

Throes, Throws

Throes means a severe spasm of pain or a condition of struggling.
*We're in the **throes** of remodeling our house for the first time.*

Throws means propels, hurls, or flings.
*The news of the profit loss **throws** a new light on the investment.*

Through, Thru

Though it is quite common, **thru** is a nonstandard word and should be avoided. Use **through** instead.

Throughway, Thruway

Thruway, meaning an expressway, is the more common word. It is derived from the words *through* and *highway*.

Thus, Thusly

Thusly is a nonstandard word. Avoid its use.

Tidbit, Titbit

Tidbit is preferred in American usage.

Tide me over, Tie me over

Tide me over, which means to help one survive a scarcity of some resource, is the correct expression. The phrase refers to a swelling tide, which can carry a small boat over an obstacle without requiring effort on the boat's part.
*This job will **tide me over** financially until I find a better one.*

Till, Until

Though considered less formal, the word **till** is acceptable shorthand for **until**.

Note that **'til**, a contraction of **until**, is an old form that has been replaced by **till**.

Timber, Timbre

Timber refers to cut wood and, figuratively, to qualify for a position.
The **timber** *company worked on replanting trees all spring.*
The new trainee has management **timber**.

Timbre refers to the quality of sound.
The young choir voices have great range and beautiful **timbre**.

Tint, Hue, Shade

See entry for **Hue, Shade, Tint**.

Titillate, Titivate

Titillate means to stimulate, tickle, or arouse pleasantly.
The spicy Buffalo chicken wings always **titillate** *our taste buds.*

Titivate means adorn or spruce up.
Hand-painted murals of famous jazz musicians **titivate** *the walls.*

Titled, Entitled

See entry for **Entitled, Titled**.

Toe the line, Tow the line

Toe the line, meaning to conform to stated standards, is the correct expression and is equivalent to *toe the mark*. The phrase refers to two things: the starting mark in a foot race (the runners must *toe the line*), and the center line in a boxing ring where boxers stand and go toe to toe.
Pressure is building on the other companies to **toe the line** *on the new environmental regulations.*

Tongue and cheek, Tongue in cheek

Tongue in cheek is the correct phrase (meaning kidding). It derives from the practice of putting one's tongue into one's cheek to keep from laughing at an inappropriate moment.
*Pat wrote a lighthearted, **tongue-in-cheek** article about his college experiences.*

Tortuous, Torturous

Tortuous means winding or crooked.
*The bus took a **tortuous** route getting to the concert venue.*

Torturous means causing pain.
*The steep mountain path is quite **torturous** to our legs and feet.*

Toward, Towards

Toward is preferred in American usage.

Track home, Tract home

Tract home is the correct phrase. It refers to a mass-produced house that has a common construction method and design.
Tract homes continue to be popular in many areas of the town.

Transient, Transitory

Transient means brief or fleeting (it usually applies to people).
*Mr. Dracon and Mr. Sasnowitz are **transient** guests at this hotel.*

Transitory means **transient** but usually applies to events.
*Don't worry, the noisy circus is **transitory**.*

Translator, Interpeter

*See entry for **Interpreter, Translator**.*

Translucent, Transparent, Opaque

*See entry for **Opaque, Translucent, Transparent**.*

*The vaudeville **troupe** entertained the **troops**.*

Troop, Troupe

Troop is a group of people or animals.
*A **troop** of new students is attending orientation this week.*

Troupe is a company of actors or performers.
*The Ithaca College Trombone **Troupe** was started in 1982.*

Trooper, Trouper

A **trooper** is a mounted soldier or police officer, or a state police officer.
*The **trooper** told the new drivers to always wear seatbelts.*

Trouper is a member of a group of actors or performers. The idiom, "He's a real trouper" means the person contributes to his team or group.
*John is a real **trouper** — he played today despite a broken arm.*

Trustee, Trusty

Trustee is someone entrusted to manage the property of others.
*Mary Jane is the public guardian and **trustee** of their estate.*

Trusty is a trustworthy prisoner who has special privileges.
*The dependable **trusty** was given a new job in the prison's library.*

Try and, Try to

Try to remember that **try to** is the correct phrase.
*We **try to** negotiate large advances for all of our clients.*

Turban, Turbine

Turban is a close-fitting hat consisting of material wound around a small inner cap. **Turbine** is a machine with blades or rotors that are driven by the pressure of fluid, steam, or gas.

Turbid, Turgid

Turbid means muddy, opaque, or unclear.
*The large mountain lake appears **turbid** after the heavy rainfall.*

Turgid means swollen or pompous.
*Steve's abdominal area is **turgid** and sensitive from the surgery.*
*The radio personality has a **turgid** style of talking to his guests.*

Turn into, Turn to

Turn into means to transform something.
*Contrary to popular belief, muscles never **turn into** fat.*

Turn to means to seek advice or solace from, or to go to a certain page in a book.
*Dissatisfied with his scores, Bill **turned to** his pro for advice.*
*The professor asked the physics class to **turn to** page 12.*

Type, Click, Press

*See entry for **Click, Press, Type**.*

Typhoon, Hurricane
See entry for **Hurricane, Typhoon.**

Tyrannical yolk, Tyrannical yoke
Tyrannical yoke, meaning a tyrant's aggressive power, is the correct phrase.

*They freed themselves from their leader's **tyrannical yoke**.*

U

Writers take words seriously — perhaps the last professional class that does.

– John Updike

Ulterior, Alterior
See entry for **Alterior, Ulterior**.

Ultimate, Penultimate
See entry for **Penultimate, Ultimate**.

Ultimately, Eventually
See entry for **Eventually, Ultimately**.

Unalienable, Inalienable
Either word is correct, but **inalienable** is more common today.

Unaware, Unawares
Unaware is an adjective that means not being aware of something.
*The organizers are **unaware** of the inclement weather forecast.*

Unawares is an adverb meaning *by surprise* or *unexpectedly*.
*The inclement weather caught the picnic organizers **unawares**.*

Unbeknown, Unbeknownst
Either spelling is acceptable.

Unbelievable
This is a much overused word. It actually means *too improbable to believe* rather than its common misuse of *good*.
*The festival offers **good** (not **unbelievable**) apple pies every fall.*
*To them, the UFO story of Roswell, New Mexico is **unbelievable**.*

Uncharted territory, Unchartered territory
Uncharted territory is the correct phrase.

Unconscience, Unconscious
Unconscience is not a word.

Under way, Underway
Either spelling is acceptable.

Undo, Undue
Undo means to reverse something.
*It will take much rain to **undo** the damage caused by the drought.*
Undue means inappropriate or excessive.
*They should be quiet and refrain from any **undue** criticism.*

Undoubtably, Undoubtedly
Undoubtably is not a word.

Unequivocably, Unequivocally
Unequivocably is not a word.

Unhealthful, Unhealthy
*See entry for **Healthful, Healthy.***

Unilateral, Bilateral, Multilateral
*See entry for **Bilateral, Multilateral, Unilateral.***

Uninterested, Disinterested
*See entry for **Disinterested, Uninterested.***

United Kingdom, British Isles, Great Britain
*See entry for **British Isles, Great Britain, United Kingdom.***

University, College
*See entry for **College, University**.*

Unloosen, Loosen
Loosen is the correct word. The *un* is not needed.

Unorganized, Disorganized
*See entry for **Disorganized, Unorganized**.*

Unreadable, Illegible
*See entry for **Illegible, Unreadable**.*

Unsatisfied, Dissatisfied
*See entry for **Dissatisfied, Unsatisfied**.*

Unsoluble, Unsolvable
Both words mean not easily solved. **Unsoluble** can also mean something is not soluble in a liquid.
*The corporation continues to have **unsoluble** (or **unsolvable**) quality problems.*

Unthaw, Thaw
*See entry for **Thaw, Unthaw**.*

Unthinkable, Inconceivable
*See entry for **Inconceivable, Unthinkable**.*

Until, Till
*See entry for **Till, Until**.*

Unwanted, Unwonted
Unwanted means not wanted.
*Occasionally we experience **unwanted** e-mails and phone calls.*

Unwonted means out of the ordinary or unusual.
*At the party, the children were in an **unwonted** state of excitement when they learned a clown was coming.*

Upmost, Outmost, Utmost
See entry for *Outmost, Upmost, Utmost.*

Upward, Upwards
Upward is preferred in American usage.

Urban, Urbane
Urban refers to a city.
*A good example of **urban** sprawl is Las Vegas, Nevada.*

Urbane means polished or smooth, as in a person's demeanor.
*The diplomat's **urbane** and polite manner impresses everyone.*

Use to, Used to
Used to is the correct phrase.
*Up until a year ago, we **used to** watch that TV drama regularly.*

V

I know many books which have bored their readers, but I know of none which has done real evil.

– Voltaire

Varied, Various

Varied is the past tense of *vary.*
*The chef **varied** the vegetables in the salad according to the season.*

Various means distinct, diverse, or of many different kinds.
*The company officers come from **various** backgrounds.*

Venal, Venial

Venal means susceptible to corruption, dishonesty, or bribery.
*The candidate didn't commit the **venal** offense of bribing voters.*

Venial means easily excused or forgiven.
*Eating meat on Fridays was once a **venial** sin to Catholics.*

Veneer, Venire

Veneer refers to a very thin layer of material or a superficial manner.
*We applied a **veneer** of walnut to the ugly pine table.*
*Their dissatisfaction was disguised by a **veneer** of friendliness.*

Venire is the panel of prospective jurors from which a jury is selected.
*Ten members of the **venire** received instructions from the court.*

Veracious, Voracious

Veracious means completely truthful or accurate.
*When the **veracious** child speaks, never doubt her honesty.*

Voracious means having an insatiable appetite.
*Since age 10, Tim has been a **voracious** reader of comics.*
*Among children, the demand for chocolate is **voracious**.*

Verbage, Verbiage
Verbiage is the correct word.

Verbal, Oral
See entry for ***Oral, Verbal.***

Verse, Stanza
See entry for ***Stanza, Verse.***

Vial, Vile
Vial is a small closable container usually for liquids.
The lab technician put the remaining liquid in a small glass ***vial.***

Vile means despicable, repulsive, or disgustingly bad.
We experienced ***vile*** *weather during our Alaskan cruise.*

Vicious, Viscose, Viscous
Vicious refers to being savage or cruel.
The mean dog displayed ***vicious*** *behavior toward the jogger.*

Viscose refers to a thick organic liquid used in the making of rayon and cellophane.
The dress uses a 100-percent ***viscose*** *fabric for a light, cool feel.*

Viscous refers to a thick or gummy liquid that is hard to pour.
Typical ***viscous*** *liquids are molasses, honey, oil, and syrup.*

Vicious circle, Vicious cycle
Vicious circle is the correct phrase.
Last year she went through a ***vicious circle*** *of changing jobs.*

Vigorish, Vigorous
Vigorish refers to interest or fees paid to a lender.
Standard ***vigorish*** *charges of 10 percent are figured into the amount due.*

Vigorous means energetic, robust, or strong.
Vigorous *exercise can decrease the risk of heart disease.*

*The **vicious** dog lapped up the **viscous** honey.*

Vigorous, Rigorous
*See entry for **Rigorous, Vigorous**.*

Villain, Villein
Villain is a bad person.
*Every James Bond film has at least one **villain** for 007 to catch.*

Villein was a feudal serf in medieval Europe.
Villeins are frequently mentioned in the Domesday Book.

Viola, Voila

A **viola** is a flower or a stringed musical instrument. **Voila** is a French expression that means *behold* or *look there.*

Visa, Passport

See entry for **Passport, Visa.**

Vocal chords, Vocal cords

Vocal cords is the correct phrase.

Vocation, Evocation, Avocation

See entry for **Avocation, Evocation, Vocation.**

Vouch, Avow

See entry for **Avow, Vouch.**

W

A new word is like a wild animal you have caught. You must learn its ways and break it before you can use it.

– H.G. Wells

Wane, Wax

Wane means to gradually decrease in strength or size.
*Their enthusiasm for our idea is definitely beginning to **wane**.*

Wax means to increase in size or strength.
*Our interest in the house started to **wax** when we saw the huge kitchen, but it subsided when we saw the moldy basement.*

Wangle, Wrangle

Wangle means to gain by trickery or contrivance.
*He **wangled** a job for which he had no qualifications.*

Wrangle means to argue or debate something angrily.
*The two coaches **wrangled** over the umpire's call.*

Wrangle also means herding or tending saddle horses.
*Paul has been **wrangling** horses in Virginia for many years now.*

Warrantee, Warranty

Warrantee is the person to whom a **warranty** is given.
*The dealer gave the **warrantee** the required forms to complete.*

Warranty is a promise to repair or replace a faulty product.
*Vehicles under a factory **warranty** will be repaired at no charge.*

Wary, Weary

Wary means cautious or watchful.
*She and John are **wary** about replacing their insurance policy.*

Weary means fatigued or tired.
*The players are **weary** after a long week of overtime matches.*

Waver, Waiver

Waver means to vacillate or be indecisive.
*Kevin says he will not **waver** on the issue of past-due royalties.*

If you sign a **waiver**, you relinquish a right, privilege, or claim.
*Jim signed a **waiver** of his right to sue for past-due royalties.*

Wean, Ween

Wean means to cause to give up something.
*The doctor is trying to **wean** him from his daily cigarettes.*

Ween means to think, suppose, or imagine something.
*We are asking students to **ween** new ideas for the school play.*

Well, Good

*See entry for **Good, Well**.*

Wench, Winch

Wench is a girl or young woman, often a servant.
*The kitchen **wench** brought the prince his dinner.*

Winch is a device that lifts or pulls heavy objects.
*The tractor was equipped with a **winch** to pull out tree stumps.*

Went, Gone

*See entry for **Gone, Went**.*

We're, Were

We're is a contraction for *we are*.
*To increase our chances, **we're** applying to many good colleges.*

Were is a past tense form of the verb *be*.
*Bill and Tom **were** applying to many colleges on the West Coast.*

Westward, Westwards

Westward is preferred in American usage.

Wet your appetite, Whet your appetite

Whet your appetite (from *whetstone*) is correct. It means to sharpen your appetite.
*I hope the menu selections **whet your appetite.***

When and if

Avoid this colloquial expression in formal writing.
*If (not **when and if**) the budget is approved, you will be trained.*

Whence, Thence, Hence

*See entry for **Hence, Thence, Whence**.*

Whereas, Although

*See entry for **Although, Whereas**.*

Which, That

*See entry for **That, Which**.*

Whiskey, Whisky

The preferred spelling in the United States and Ireland is **whiskey**. Great Britain and Canada use **whisky**.

Whither, Wither

Whither means *to what place.*
*"**Whither** thou goest, I will go."* (Ruth 1:16)

Wither means to dry up or shrivel from lack of moisture.
*The plants in the green house **wither** without sufficient water.*

Who, Whom

Though some people today tend to ignore this distinction, careful writers and speakers retain the distinction of nominative and objective pronoun case.

To choose the correct pronoun of **who** or **whom**, you need to recognize whether the pronoun is being used as a subject (the nominative form) or an object (the objective form). **Who** is

nominative (for subjects), and **whom** is objective (for objects).
Who (subject) left the party last?
Whom (object) should the invitation go to?

Try substituting a personal pronoun (*he, she, him, her, they, them*) in place of **who** or **whom**. If *he, she,* or *they* fits, use **who**.
Who is the junior Senator from that state?
She is the junior Senator from that state.

If *him, her,* or *them* fits, use **whom**.
The outcome could depend on whom?
The outcome could depend on them.

Trick example:
The gift must be returned by whoever bought it.

Here the whole clause *whoever bought it* is the object of the preposition *by*. But *whoever* remains nominative because it is the subject of that clause.

Who's, Whose

Who's is the contraction for *who is.*
Who's that person you are recommending for the position?

Who's can also mean *who has.*
Who's been sending money to the charity anonymously?

Whose is the possessive form of *who.*
Whose report card shows the most improvement from last year?

Will, Shall

*See entry for **Shall, Will**.*

Wimbleton, Wimbledon

Wimbledon is the correct name of the tennis location in England.

Win-loss, Won-loss

The correct expression is **won-loss**.
*The team had an impressive **won-loss** record last year.*

With regard to, With regards to

With regard to, without an *s*, is the correct phrase. Note that often you can substitute words such as *on, about,* or *concerning*.
*He notified us **with regard to** (on, about, concerning) the cost.*

Without further adieu, Without further ado

Without further ado is the correct phrase.
*Now, **without further ado**, here are the answers to the quiz.*

World Wide Web

Like the word *Internet*, the phrase **World Wide Web** is always capitalized.

World-renown, World-renowned

World-renowned is the correct phrase.
*The **world-renowned** singer was known for his gifts to charity.*

Worse comes to worse, worst comes to worst

Though illogical, **worst comes to worst** is the correct phrase.
*If **worst comes to worst** you can apply for a refund.*

Would have, Would of

Would have is the correct phrase.
*If you had read the book, you **would have** known the answer.*

Wrack, Rack

See entry for **Rack, Wrack**.

Wreak, Wreck

Wreak means to cause something, almost always trouble.
*Unexpected expenses **wreak** havoc on the department budget.*

Wreck means to destroy something.
*Unexpected expenses **wrecked** our organization's budget.*

Wreaking havoc, Reeking havoc
Wreaking havoc is the correct phrase.
*The unusually bad weather is **wreaking havoc** in some states.*

Wreath, Wreathe
Wreath refers to flowers or other things intertwined into a circle.
*Pat and Russ chose a holiday **wreath** for the centerpiece.*

Wreathe means to proceed on a repeatedly curving course.
*The smoke continues to **wreathe** upward through the trees.*

Wretch, Retch
*See entry for **Retch, Wretch**.*

Wright, Right
*See entry for **Right, Wright**.*

Y

Think like a wise man but communicate in the language of the people.
– William Butler Yeats

Yoke, Yolk

Yoke is a crosspiece holding two things together.
*The ox with the plow has a wooden **yoke** around its neck.*

Yolk is the yellow part of an egg.
*The **yolk** of the egg contains most of the protein.*

Yore, Your, You're

Yore is an old word meaning *time long past.*
*The days of **yore** were filled with many courageous heroes.*

Your is the possessive form of *you.*
*The application form is on **your** desk.*

You're is a contraction of *you are.*
*If **you're** interested, they post new job listings every Sunday.*

About the Author

Dave Dowling has been a technical writer, editor, and instructor for over 25 years. His experience includes commercial and government work for large corporations.

Earlier, Dave worked in radio syndication in Los Angeles, where he assisted in the production of nationally syndicated radio shows *American Top 40* and *American Country Countdown*. Today he is president of *Write On Course, LLC* (www.writeoncourse.com), a company that specializes in business and technical writing seminars.

He was recently interviewed by *NBC Nightly News* for a segment on business writing. He is also a member of the *Society for Technical Communication* and the author of *Steve Reeves – His Legacy in Films*.

The author holds an M.S. from the University at Albany, N.Y. and a B.A. from the State University College at Potsdam, N.Y. He lives in Owego, New York with his wife Mary and son Tim.

Bibliography

Writing Guides

The Careful Writer: A Modern Guide to English Usage, Theodore M. Bernstein. New York: Atheneum, 1977.

College English and Communication, Marie M. Stewart and Kenneth Zimmer. 4th ed. New York: McGraw-Hill, 1982.

The Columbia Guide to Standard American English, Kenneth G. Wilson. New York: Columbia University Press, 1993.

The Elements of Style, William Strunk Jr., and E.B. White. 4th ed. New York: Longman, 2000.

Good Grammar Made Easy, Martin Steinmann and Michael Keller. New York: Gramercy Books, 1999.

The Handbook of Good English, Edward D. Johnson. New York: Facts On File Publications, 1982.

Handbook for Writers, Celia Millward. New York: Holt, Rinehart and Winston, 1983.

Harbrace College Handbook, John C. Hodges, Mary E. Whittens, Winifred B. Horner, Suzanne S. Webb, Robert K. Miller. 12th ed. New York: Harcourt Brace Jovanovich, Publishers, 1995.

The Little, Brown Handbook, H. Ramsey Fowler. Boston: Little, Brown and Company, 1980.

The Office Guide to Modern English Usage, Carol M. Barnum and Jean C. Vermes. 2nd ed. New York: MJF Books, 1991.

Put It in Writing!, Albert Joseph. New and Updated Edition. New York: McGraw-Hill, 1998.

The Random House Handbook, Frederick Crews. 6th ed. New York: Random House, 1991.

Sleeping Dogs Don't Lay, Richard Lederer and Richard Dowis. New York: St. Martin's Press, 1999.

Strictly Speaking, Edwin Newman. New York: Warner Books, 1974.

Woe Is I, Patricia T. O'Conner. New York: Riverhead Books, August 1998.

The Wordwatcher's Guide to Good Writing & Grammar, Morton S. Freeman. Cincinnati: Writer's Digest Books, 1990.

The Write Way, Richard Lederer and Richard Dowis. New York: Pocket Books, 1995.

The Writer's Art, James J. Kilpatrick. Kansas City: Andrews and McMeel, June 1993.

Dictionaries and Style Guides

American Century Dictionary. New York: Reissue. Warner Books, 1996.

American Heritage Dictionary of the English Language. 4th ed. New York: Houghton Mifflin Company, 2000.

Associated Press Stylebook and Libel Manual. Revised and Updated Edition. New York: Perseus Publishing, 1998.

Chicago Manual of Style. 15th ed. Chicago: Univ. of Chicago Press, 2003.

Merriam-Webster's Collegiate Dictionary. 11th ed. Springfield, MA: Merriam-Webster, 2003.

Oxford American Desk Dictionary and Thesaurus. 2nd ed. New York: Berkley Publishing Group, 2001.

Random House Webster's College Dictionary. Indexed edition. New York: Random House, 2000.

Random House Webster's Unabridged Dictionary. 2nd ed. New York: Random House, 2001.

Webster's New World College Dictionary. 4th ed. New York: Macmillan Reference Books, 2003.

Webster's New World Roget's Thesaurus A-Z. 4th ed. New York: Wiley, John & Sons, Inc., 1999.